on track ...
Barclay James Harvest

every album, every song

Keith & Monika Domone

SONICBOND

sonicbondpublishing.com

Sonicbond Publishing Limited
www.sonicbondpublishing.co.uk
Email: info@sonicbondpublishing.co.uk

First Published in the United Kingdom 2020
First Published in the United States 2020

British Library Cataloguing in Publication Data:
A Catalogue record for this book is available from the British Library

ISBN 978-1-78952-067-5

Typeset in ITC Garamond & ITC Avant Garde
Printed and bound in England

Graphic design and typesetting: Full Moon Media

Acknowledgements

With grateful thanks to Stephen Lambe and Sonicbond for commissioning the book, and to Theo Verstrael for suggesting it in the first place!

We'd also like to acknowledge the invaluable input provided by John Lees, Jeremy Smith and Mark Powell.

Cover photo: Mike Muller

On behalf of all fans of Barclay James Harvest, our gratitude goes to John, Les, Mel and Woolly, and all who have contributed to the enduring music of Barclay James Harvest over the last fifty years. Here's to the next half-century!

This book is dedicated to the memory of Woolly Wolstenholme and Mel Pritchard.

Would you like to write for Sonicbond Publishing?

We are mainly a music publisher, but we also occasionally publish in other genres including film and television. At Sonicbond Publishing we are always on the look-out for authors, particularly for our two main series, On Track and Decades.

Mixing fact with in depth analysis, the On Track series examines the entire recorded work of a particular musical artist or group. All genres are considered from easy listening and jazz to 60s soul to 90s pop, via rock and metal.

The Decades series singles out a particular decade in an artist or group's history and focuses on that decade in more detail than may be allowed in the On Track series.

While professional writing experience would, of course, be an advantage, the most important qualification is to have real enthusiasm and knowledge of your subject. First-time authors are welcomed, but the ability to write well in English is essential.

Sonicbond Publishing has distribution throughout Europe and North America, and all our books are also published in E-book form. Authors will be paid a royalty based on sales of their book. Further details about our books are available from www.sonicbondpublishing.com. To contact us, complete the contact form there or email info@sonicbondpublishing.co.uk

on track ...

Barclay James Harvest

Contents

Introduction

Barclay James Harvest are something of an enigma within the world of popular music. Variously categorised as everything from folk to progressive, rock and pop, the band ploughed their own furrow for three decades, outside of the mainstream and largely unknown beyond the cognoscenti in their home territory of the United Kingdom, whilst achieving megastar status in Germany, Switzerland and, briefly, France. During those thirty years, they notched up sales in excess of ten million albums, qualified for numerous silver, gold and platinum sales awards, had number one albums and singles and played to millions of enthusiastic concertgoers across Europe, whilst remaining widely regarded as a 'cult' band.

Rooted in the blues and soul scene of their home town of Oldham, Lancashire, in the north-west of England, the group was formed in the summer of 1967 from the remnants of two semi-professional outfits: The Blues Keepers, featuring Stuart 'Woolly' Wolstenholme and John Lees, and Heart and Soul and the Wickeds, which included Les Holroyd, Mel Pritchard and Rod Buckley in the line-up. The departure of original singer Rod Buckley, in August 1967, reduced the new band to a stable quartet comprising Lees, Wolstenholme, Holroyd and Pritchard. The band were discovered very early in their career by local boutique owner John Crowther, who became their manager and set them up in Preston House, an old coaching inn by the village of Diggle, high on windswept Saddleworth Moor. The group set to work writing and recording demos of their original songs and released their first single, 'Early Morning', in April 1968 on EMI's Parlophone label.

This led to a contract with EMI's new 'progressive' label, Harvest, for whom they would record four albums over the next four years, including the beautiful *Once Again* – well received at the time, particularly the timeless 'Mocking Bird', and now regarded as a classic. Critical acclaim and a small but growing following were not enough to pay the bills, though, particularly when the band ran up large debts by touring and recording with their own symphony orchestra, and in December 1973 Barclay James Harvest parted ways with the Harvest label and signed a new deal with Polydor Records.

The change of label heralded an upswing in the band's fortunes as they released a series of superb albums, from 1974's *Everyone Is Everybody Else* through to *XII* in 1978, and enjoyed steadily growing success at home and then, increasingly, in continental Europe. 1977's *Gone To Earth* became a fixture in the German album charts and turned them into overnight superstars, more than a decade after they had started out.

What many fans regard as the golden age of the band was brought to an end by the departure of Woolly Wolstenholme in 1979, due to dissatisfaction with his role in the group and the more commercial path which their music was taking – and then there were three. The remaining members resolved to continue as a trio, augmented by guest musicians when necessary, and through the 1980s broke attendance records for concert tours in Germany and Switzerland, as well as topping the charts with albums like *Turn Of The Tide*, *Victims Of Circumstance* and *Berlin (A Concert For The People)*. The latter is a record of Barclay James Harvest's biggest triumph; a free concert performed on 30 August 1980 on the steps of the historic Reichstag parliament building in Berlin, which was attended by a huge crowd of an estimated quarter of a million people. Another highlight was the first major open-air concert given by a Western rock band in East Germany, on 14 July 1988 in East Berlin's Treptower Park, and attended by around 170,000 fans.

Barclay James Harvest continued to record and tour in the 1990s, but increasing tensions within the band over their preferred musical direction and methods of working slowed their output to three studio albums in seven years, and their star began to fade. A 'sabbatical' announced after the relatively poor sales of 1997's *River Of Dreams* CD and associated tour became permanent, and Barclay James Harvest split into two bands. John Lees chose to team up again with a returning Woolly Wolstenholme, following which Les Holroyd conceived his own vision of BJH, aided by Mel Pritchard.

Tragedy struck twice in the twenty-first century with the untimely death of Mel Pritchard in January 2004 and the suicide of Woolly Wolstenholme in December 2010. However, both John Lees and Les Holroyd remain active to this day, playing songs from the extensive Barclay James Harvest back catalogue to enthusiastic crowds, as well as performing and recording new material.

The primary focus of this book is the body of work created by the original Barclay James Harvest up to 1997, with every album and song covered in depth. There is also room for a peek into the related solo works and those of John Lees' and Les Holroyd's bands, which continue to fly the BJH flag to this day. As John Lees put it in his 1993 song 'Once More', 'They'll never kill the mockingbird' ...

Barclay James Harvest (1970)

Personnel:
John Lees: vocals, lead guitar
Les Holroyd: vocals, bass guitar, keyboards
Woolly Wolstenholme: vocals, keyboards
Mel Pritchard: drums and percussion
The Barclay James Harvest Orchestra, conducted by Resident Musical Director Robert Godfrey
Recorded at E.M.I Studios, Abbey Road, November 1969 to January 1970
Producer: Norman Smith
Engineer: Phil McDonald
Record Label: Harvest (UK), Sire (US)
UK release date: 5 June 1970, U.S. release date November 1970

Barclay James Harvest's recording career got off to a slow start, with only a brace of singles ('Early Morning'/'Mr. Sunshine' and 'Brother Thrush'/'Poor Wages') being released in 1968 and 1969 respectively, but behind the scenes, they were busy writing and recording demos of many original songs, as well as performing a lot of live shows. By November 1969, they were ready to begin work on their debut LP, and arrived at the iconic studios in Abbey Road in North-West London, then known simply as E.M.I. Studios, on the 8th of that month. They had already had a taste of their surroundings the previous May while recording 'Brother Thrush'. However, this was to be an altogether much more ambitious project, involving an orchestra comprising music students from the Royal College Of Music and The Royal Academy, assembled and conducted by Robert Godfrey, the band's new Musical Arranger. The plan proved over-ambitious, as the inexperienced students were out of their depth in a professional recording studio with an equally untried conductor, and although 'Dark Now My Sky' was acceptable, the other recordings were unusable. Fortunately, a classical musician of Godfrey's acquaintance named Martyn Ford already had his own very capable orchestra, made up of the best students from the London music colleges and known as The London Symphonia. Renamed The Barclay James Harvest Orchestra for the occasion, they stepped into the breach, with Ford as leader of the orchestra.

The entire album was recorded in around eighty hours, using only two eight-track tape recorders. Drummer Mel Pritchard told *Beat Instrumental* magazine the following year,

> We had drums, bass, Mellotron, piano, organ, double-tracked guitar, orchestra, vocals and effects to go on. It took time to work out how to do it, because we didn't want to lump the bass and drums together, and we also wanted the stereo effect of the guitars, so in the end we used two eight-tracks.

Given the relatively short time allowed for recording, and the hugely ambitious idea of using a full orchestra on a band's debut album, the results were surprisingly good, but the band members weren't entirely satisfied. As Woolly put it nearly twenty years later:

> Generally, the album wasn't as successful as it could have been – it was rather overblown. It seemed to be rather a pre-emptive strike, a rehearsal for the real thing.

Flawed though it may have been, the band's debut album set out their stall as an ambitious fusion of folk, rock and classical music, it was warmly received by critics and influential radio DJs such as John Peel and Alan Freeman, and paved the way for greater things to come.

Sleeve Design

Mixing of the album was completed on 26 February 1970 and ready to be launched in March, but the release was held up because the band weren't keen on the Harvest label's plan to use design studio Hipgnosis to create the album's cover. Woolly Wolstenholme, in particular, felt that Hipgnosis tended to apply their own identity regardless of its appropriateness to the artist concerned. The band got their way, choosing instead a kaleidoscopic, repeating stained glass butterfly image designed by Ian Latimer on the outside of a lavish gatefold sleeve. Inside the sleeve were sepia-tinted photographs of the four band members taken by Richard Dunkley at *The Hanging Gate* pub in Diggle and at Preston House. Curiously, the names of the individual musicians of Barclay James Harvest are not shown anywhere on the sleeve or record label of the original LP, but two other individuals are credited with 'Special thanks to Jim and Jim'. Jim Tetlow was the band's road manager and sound engineer, whilst James Litherland, who played some percussion on 'Taking Some Time On', was another Lancashire lad and the guitarist and vocalist in the band Colosseum.

'Taking Some Time On' (Barclay James Harvest)

Written by John Lees and with Les Holroyd taking on lead vocals, the album opener was one of the last of the album's songs to be recorded, on 26 January 1970, fulfilling a need for an attention-grabbing opener. From the raw opening riff, inspired by the double-tracked lead guitar sound of Cream's 'Politician', it rocks along nicely with the band playing alone, without orchestral accompaniment. The lyrics, apparently espousing a simple idealism and referring to 'hidden meanings of the mind', were, said John many years later, not intended to be taken seriously. 'It was a hippy song', he said, 'Very tongue in cheek.' He rated it as the second favourite of his own songs on the album, and in the summer of 2011, it was dusted off again for John Lees' Barclay James Harvest's appearance at the High Voltage Festival in London, going down so well that it subsequently made regular appearances in the band's live shows. The delay in the release of the album had scuppered plans for a version of 'Good Love Child' to be issued as a single in advance of the LP, and instead a new single mix of 'Taking Some Time On' was created, rather belatedly, at Abbey Road on 10 August and released to the public on the 28th of that month, by which time the album had already been out for the best part of three months. Unsurprisingly the single, released as HAR 5003 and backed with the album version of 'The Iron Maiden', made little impact.

'Mother Dear' (Barclay James Harvest)

Another John Lees song, 'Mother Dear' offers quite a contrast to the album opener: a gothic tale from the same arcane realms as the short stories of Edgar Allan Poe or medieval poems like 'True Thomas', the song concerns ghostly apparitions and a visitation from the grim reaper in the night and dates back to 1967. An early demo recording featured out of tune honky-tonk bar-room piano, but, perhaps fortunately, producer Norman Smith came up with a new orchestral arrangement, in which the soaring strings and warbling brass offer a subtle counterpoint to the vaguely unsettling theme of the lyrics. Woolly Wolstenholme sings this one – John Lees later wryly suggested that he had been told that he wasn't allowed to play lead guitar and take on the lead vocal at the same time, but Woolly's memory was slightly different:

> In the early days, he didn't used to sing. That's why most of the material in the early days has me, very high profile, singing-wise, and then gradually, as people either got more confident, or saw what a bad job I was doing, they decided to do it themselves!

'The Sun Will Never Shine' (Barclay James Harvest)

The entire recording of Woolly's 'The Sun Will Never Shine' was completed on the first day of recording, 8 November, including all of the orchestral parts! The gentle Mellotron intro gives way to Woolly's reflective verse, and then everyone comes crashing in on the chorus to create the first hint of the epic fusion of rock and classical sounds which would become a Barclay James Harvest trademark over the next few years. John Lees was a big fan, rating it as his favourite song on the album: 'It gave me a big high, and still sounds great!' Woolly himself described it as 'a kind of antidote to 'Mr. Sunshine', which was about hiding from the bright light of day, not about drugs! 'The Sun Will Never Shine' and 'Ra' have a similar theme.' A 1969 solo demo recording made by Woolly at Preston House, and included in a deluxe box set edition of the album released by Esoteric Recordings in 2018, shows that the song as originally conceived was a good bit faster, and given a country-ish feel by the acoustic guitar accompaniment. The song was played live before the album was recorded, naturally without the minimal orchestral accompaniment, and subsequently became a regular in the live set at concerts, whether the band happened to be appearing with or without the orchestra.

'When the World Was Woken' (Barclay James Harvest)

The only Les Holroyd composition on the album sees the composer musing on attitudes to life, the thoughtful, introspective lyric a gentle wakeup call and exhortation to mankind to be positive and 'live together, with one triumphant cry'. Unfortunately, the rather rushed nature of the recording impacted this song more than most on the album, with the meandering and unsubtle orchestral arrangement, including a direct lift of a fanfare from Handel's *Water Music*, too high in the mix and constantly threatening to overwhelm Les's voice. The performance, too, was less than perfect. As Les later recalled,

> I remember writing all the melody lines for that on a Hammond. The singing was all over the place, but in those days you didn't have the luxury of going back and doing it all again!

The Hammond organ parts he mentions bring to mind the grandeur of Procol Harum, required listening at Preston House in those days, but the overall effect is, sadly, less disciplined. The general chaos even extended to the song's title: at the time of first recording it was noted on the Abbey Road log sheets as simply 'Les Untitled', before becoming 'When The World Was Broken' and finally 'When The World Was Woken'. None of these was correct, as the actual title Les decided upon was 'When The World Has Woken', as sung in the lyrics, but the mistake wasn't picked up, and the piece became known as 'When The World Was Woken' for all time!

'Good Love Child' (Barclay James Harvest)

More successful, and more representative of Barclay James Harvest live shows of the time, was the band-only rocker, 'Good Love Child', composed by John Lees and sung by Les Holroyd. Lyrically simple, it's a singalong, typical sixties period piece where the band are clearly having fun, bouncing along, propelled by Mel Pritchard's exuberant drumming and Les's driving bass, with John's guitar solos linking the verses and choruses. At over five minutes long it may outstay its welcome slightly on record, but in the live context that would have made perfect sense. It's the least ambitious piece on the album, but provides some variety and was never intended to be more than, as John put it, 'Just an out-and-out rock and roll song.' Early on in the recording sessions, it was decided that 'Good Love Child' was catchy and commercial enough to be released as a single, and plans were made to issue it in the New Year of 1970, but the idea was abandoned when the issues over the cover design caused the album's release to be delayed until June.

'The Iron Maiden' (Barclay James Harvest)

A complete contrast now, with Woolly Wolstenholme's delicate composition, 'The Iron Maiden'. Woolly described it as 'a folk song in a kind of 'Olde Englishe' way', reflecting a kind of medieval feel, but then rather spoilt the effect by confessing that 'The song was actually about a rather obnoxious girl I knew who was nicknamed Behemoth!' Clearly, the unreal girl who didn't feel had a big impact on Woolly, inspiring one of his most beautiful and enduring songs. Here the arrangement is sympathetic and enhances, rather than drowning, the vocal. The song received television exposure when it was featured on BBC 2's music showcase, *Disco 2*, the precursor to the *Old Grey*

Whistle Test produced by Rowan Ayers (the father of singer-songwriter Kevin Ayers) and presented by Tommy Vance, accompanied by film of Brunel's iron-hulled steamship, SS Great Britain. Woolly himself was clearly fond of the song, returning to it in live performances with his own band, Mæstoso, in the early eighties, and again when he got back together with John for the *Nexus* album and associated concerts. His bandmates, too, held it in high regard, with John Lees' Barclay James Harvest performing it as a tribute to Woolly at a 50th anniversary celebration of BJH's music in 2018 and at subsequent concerts.

'Dark Now My Sky' (Barclay James Harvest)

The pièce de résistance of the album was saved for its closing track, the grand finale of 'Dark Now My Sky'. Penned by John Lees, the song was inspired by the classic 1962 environmental text, *The Silent Spring* by Rachel Carson, an American zoologist. The lyrics include the title of the book and that of one of its chapters, 'And No Birds Sing', which is itself a quote from the Keats poem, *La Belle Dame Sans Merci*. First recorded in 1968 for a John Peel session as a sub-four-minute song with Woolly taking the lead vocal and a completely different chorus, it was now reinvented as a twelve-minute epic, showcasing the talents of the orchestra and band at their peak. A portentous drum beat augurs the phrasing of the first line of the lyrics and introduces Woolly hamming it up in his best 'Shakespearean' voice (inspired by Peter Sellers' classic parody declaiming The Beatles' 'A Hard Day's Night'!). Woolly got into the role by donning a cape and an artificial humpback ... As if that weren't over the top enough, it's followed by maniacal laughter from Robert Godfrey before the brooding orchestral introduction takes over, then John's lead guitar comes screaming in to announce the main melody. Les Holroyd sings the lead vocal on the album recording, and both Les and John rate it as their favourite track from the debut album. In truth, it's the one piece on the album where the band and orchestra really gel, the orchestral parts becoming an integral part of the composition instead of a bolted on afterthought, turning 'Dark Now My Sky' into a *bona fide* BJH classic. The one criticism which could be levelled at it is that it's a little overblown, but it's still a magnificent achievement and an augury of great things to come. Shorn of its more fanciful embellishments, it quickly became a live favourite, a showstopper to finish both band-only and orchestral concerts on a high note.

Related Songs:

'Early Morning' (Barclay James Harvest)

Where it all began: the first-ever single by Barclay James Harvest, recorded on 14 February 1968 at Chappell Studios in London's Bond Street. The band had been much impressed by Procol Harum's 'A Whiter Shade Of Pale' the previous year and wanted to create something comparable. As Woolly put it, though, 'Whilst it was true we were moved to knock-together another 'Whiter Shade Of Pale', it became another creature with its own distinct character – thank God we didn't use a Hammond!' 'Early Morning' would prove to be unique in the entire Barclay James Harvest catalogue, as a true collaborative writing effort. John recalled, forty years later, 'We never wrote together, other than helping out on lyrics or joining songs together arrangement-wise, because our styles were so different. We only did it once – on 'Early Morning'!' Studio time was expensive in those days, and the number of takes had to be kept to an absolute minimum. Woolly remembered a slight *faux pas* on his part:

> There was an incident wherein I was doubling the lead vocal. General round of applause for a perfect take ('It's amazingly close to the original!') – when in fact, I wasn't singing!

He'd missed his cue for part of the second vocal take, so it wasn't altogether surprising that the others couldn't hear the difference between the original and the 'two-track' version ... A deal was done with EMI's Parlophone label whereby the band paid their own recording costs, but Parlophone would release the single, even though the band had not yet formally signed a contract with EMI. 'Early Morning' was released as Parlophone R 5693 on 26 April 1968, in glowing mono, as was the norm for single releases at the time, although a rather ghastly 'reprocessed stereo' version was later included on the classic budget-price compilation LP, *Early Morning Onwards*. The original mono recording can be found on numerous LP and CD compilations and on remastered CD editions of the debut album. It's a charming, Mellotron-led song, and although it didn't trouble the chart compilers, it caught the ear of influential DJ John Peel, who declared it 'a beautiful sound', and predicted, prescient as ever, that 'They're going to do great things.'

'Mr. Sunshine' (Barclay James Harvest)

The B-side of 'Early Morning' had, like the A-side, first been recorded at Strawberry Studios in Stockport for a ten minute Granada TV film broadcast at the beginning of 1968 and made by a friend, Lawrence Moore, who had also worked with Pink Floyd. The film has no commentary, and depicts the band members clowning around Preston House to a soundtrack of early demo versions of 'Early Morning', 'Washing The Dishes' and 'Mr. Sunshine', from which the film *Scene: Mr. Sunshine* took its name. Whilst 'Early Morning' was completely re-recorded at Chappell's, for the less important B-side it was decided to use the backing track of the Granada film demo, augmented with new, overdubbed vocal parts and recorder solo, played by Les. Penned by Woolly, 'Mr. Sunshine' showed a darker facet of his writing, concerning itself with depression and melancholy – the antithesis of the A-side's optimism. Another mono recording, 'Mr. Sunshine' also received the dubious benefit of a reprocessed stereo mix for the *Early Morning Onwards* compilation, whilst the original version appears on remasters of the *Barclay James Harvest* album.

'Washing The Dishes' (Barclay James Harvest)

This song has only ever appeared in DVD format, as part of the short black and white film *Scene: Mr. Sunshine*, which Granada TV broadcast in 1968. It's a jokey, vaudeville number written by Woolly Wolstenholme, influenced by the surreal 1920s jazz style of The Temperance Seven, and Lawrence Moore's suitably slapstick footage has Woolly washing the dishes, appropriately enough, at Preston House, with help from the 'children' – John, Les and Mel!

'So Tomorrow' (Barclay James Harvest)
Featured in early Barclay James Harvest live shows, 'So Tomorrow' was written by Les Holroyd and first recorded in demo form by the band at Peter Tattersall's Intercity Sound studios above the Nield & Hardy musical instrument shop in Stockport. Shortly afterwards, it was one of five songs recorded on 23 April 1968, at the BBC's Studio 1 in London's Piccadilly for a John Peel *Top Gear* radio session, with Bernie Andrews producing and Dave Tate as sound engineer. It's an upbeat, infectious number, belying the subject matter of a departed girlfriend, with Les taking the lead vocal for the verses, and John, Les and Woolly harmonising on the chorus. The song remained unreleased in any form until the BBC session recording was finally released in May 2002 on a remastered CD of the first album, and it's also included in recent Esoteric Recordings editions of the same album.

'Eden Unobtainable' (Barclay James Harvest)
Another Les Holroyd song from that first John Peel session in April 1968 was this slower reflection on the impossibility of attaining perfection in this life and the individual's insignificance in the great scheme of things. Drenched in delicious Mellotron, it's a sweet confection and very much of its time, but, like 'So Tomorrow', wouldn't see the light of day until decades later – in this case, May 1991, when a July 1968 demo recording of it made at Chappell Studios was included on the EMI compilation, *The Harvest Years*. The recording, together with 'Pools Of Blue' and 'I Can't Go On Without You' from the same recording session, had surfaced in the form of seven-inch acetate discs acquired from the original Harvest label manager, Malcolm Jones, by a Barclay James Harvest fan, Steve Hibbard, and were carefully transferred to the digital realm at Abbey Road Studios for posterity.

'I Can't Go On Without You' (Barclay James Harvest)
Joining the list of great lost Barclay James Harvest songs from the sixties is this delicate Woolly Wolstenholme lament for lost love. His fondness (and the band's) for the song is reflected in the fact that the band recorded demos of it on several occasions at Intercity and Chappell Studios, as well as including it in the April 1968 BBC session set, but still, it was consigned to obscurity, until the acetate recording of the July 1968 Chappells session was rescued for *The Harvest Years*. It's a lovely little song, with accompaniment from piano and the Mellotron providing not only the trademark string sound but also some quite convincing flute and accordion parts.

'Night' (Barclay James Harvest)
John Peel, now an enthusiastic Barclay James Harvest fan, invited them back to do another session for his *Top Gear* programme, for which they

returned to BBC Studio 1 on 30 July 1968, with Bernie Andrews once more in the producer's seat. All five of the tracks recorded that day were previously unreleased songs from the band's current live set and showed the fledgeling band rapidly developing their sound into new directions, incorporating influences from the contemporary rock and pop scene. 'Night' is a Wolstenholme rocker, with Woolly's vocals married to John Lees' driving guitar, producing a powerful track, reminiscent of Cream or the more energetic side of Love. The latter's classic *Forever Changes* album had been released the previous November, and was a firm favourite at Preston House, having a big impact on their writing, especially Woolly and John. 'Night' remained unreleased until the Peel session recording was added to the 2002 EMI remastered CD of the first album.

'Pools of Blue' (Barclay James Harvest)

Another song from that period which languished in limbo for over twenty years was 'Pools Of Blue'. A John Lees composition looking at the world from the perspective of a blind girl, it's the first known recording of John singing lead vocals, and was evidently an important song to him, as the band made five attempts to record it at Intercity, Chappells and the BBC during the course of 1968, and returned to it during Abbey Road recording sessions in the early seventies. Their plan was to offer it to EMI as the follow-up single to 'Early Morning', but the band members themselves were never entirely happy with the results. In any case, the record company declined to release any of the recordings.

John is on record as saying that it's the one song of his which he would most like to re-record, preferably with an orchestra. It's a lovely, lyrical piece, but does lack that certain spark to elevate it into the realms of the best of the band's work. Nonetheless, it still managed to play a vital role in the band's history: while working on 'Pools Of Blue', John came up with another riff, one which would become one of the defining Barclay James Harvest songs – the timeless classic, 'Mocking Bird'. An early demo of 'Pools Of Blue' appeared on *The Harvest Years*, whilst the 2018 deluxe box set of the debut album includes no less than three versions of it – two different demo recordings and the July 1968 session take broadcast by *Top Gear*.

'Need You Oh So Bad' (Barclay James Harvest)

This song, also from the second John Peel session and featured on remastered editions of the first album, is a Woolly Wolstenholme composition written in the style of one of his favourite singer-songwriters, Tim Hardin. The title is very similar to that of another song which BJH used to play live in the very early days, the blues standard 'Need Your Love So Bad', written by Mertis John Jr. in the fifties, but popularised at the time of this recording by Peter Green's Fleetwood Mac. The session take of Woolly's song sounds a little rushed, clocking in at a mere one minute and fifteen seconds, but highlights a pleasant, if inconsequential, little song on a recurring theme of a failed relationship. It's lifted by some solo descant recorder parts, played by John, a rare example of Les playing cello, and Mel's jaunty percussion.

'Small Time Town' (Barclay James Harvest)

The final song from the second Peel session was written by John and sung by Woolly, with Les harmonising on the chorus. The subject matter reminisces of childhood, a theme to which John would occasionally return over the years, but it's instructive to reflect that he was writing this at an age when he was barely out of his own childhood and already nostalgic for the back streets of Oldham. Like virtually all of the songs from the 1968 BBC radio sessions, this can be found on both the 2002 EMI remastered CD of their first album, and the 2018 Esoteric Recordings deluxe box set.

'Brother Thrush' (Barclay James Harvest)

Plans for 'Pools Of Blue' to be released as a follow-up to 'Early Morning' having come to nought, there was a long hiatus before the second single finally appeared. In the meantime, EMI had given the go-ahead for the launch of their new 'progressive' imprint, Harvest, and on 25 April 1969 Barclay James Harvest became the latest signings to the label. On 11 May they were packed off to Abbey Road with producer Norman Smith, already well-known for his work with The Beatles and The Rolling Stones, to record the new single.

'Brother Thrush' was sung by Woolly but penned by John, and is the first, if far from the last, BJH recording to explore environmental issues, predicting the eventual triumph of nature over the works of man. The difference that a top-flight recording studio and producer could make, not to mention a year's extra experience for the musicians, is apparent: much more assured than their debut, 'Brother Thrush' is an uplifting song, beautifully recorded in stereo, no less! The band was augmented for the recording by Robert Godfrey, now living with them at Preston House and working on his plans for combining group and orchestra, and he contributed organ and backing vocals to 'Brother Thrush'. The record was released on 20 June 1969, as HAR 5003 and was the third single to appear on the Harvest label.

'Poor Wages' (Barclay James Harvest)

For the B-side of the single, a favourite from their live repertoire was selected. Originally called 'Being Satisfied', and annotated thus on the Abbey Road log sheets, Woolly's song, now re-titled 'Poor Wages', is, perhaps, an even stronger song than the A-side. It had first been recorded as a demo at Intercity Sound (subsequently renamed Strawberry Studios), but now it came into its own in a state-of-the-art studio. Woolly played the lead guitar part on a Fender electric twelve-string and sang the lead vocal. At live shows, 'Being Satisfied' featured a blistering John Lees guitar solo which, sadly, wasn't included on the single recording, but was resurrected thirty-seven years later as part of the John Lees' Barclay James Harvest live set! Both sides of the single have been collected up in numerous anthologies over the years, from the fondly-remembered *Early Morning Onwards* in 1972 to the lavish 2018 debut album box set, within which listeners were treated to both remastered versions of the original recordings and brand new stereo mixes.

Once Again (1971)

Personnel:
John Lees: vocals, guitars, recorder
Les Holroyd: vocals, bass guitar, keyboards
Woolly Wolstenholme: vocals, keyboards
Mel Pritchard: drums and percussion
The Barclay James Harvest Orchestra, conducted by Resident Musical Director Robert Godfrey, orchestra leader Gavin Wright
Recorded at EMI Studios, Abbey Road, 9 October 1970 to 25 November 1970
Producer: Norman Smith
Engineer: Peter Brown
Record Label: Harvest (UK), Sire (US)
UK release date: 5 February 1971

Once the debut *Barclay James Harvest* album had finally appeared in the June of 1970, there was little time for the band to rest on their laurels. A showpiece quartet of orchestral concerts, including one at London's famous Royal Albert Hall, was followed by a series of band-only live shows through September, and then it was time to think about recording a follow-up LP. They set to work rehearsing at the Civic Hall in nearby Uppermill, where they had been given permission by the local council to rehearse for six hours a day on Thursdays and Fridays, with the proviso that the noise was kept to a reasonable level! Norman Smith and the orchestra were booked, and work began on 9 October. There was a catch to recording at the prestigious Abbey Road Studios, though. Daytime recording was fully booked for established chart acts like The Beatles, so lesser groups like Barclay James Harvest had to make do with 'off-peak' hours. As Woolly recalled, 'We would start at about 6.00 p.m. We would do the night shift there and stay at The Madison in Sussex Gardens and spend all day walking aimlessly around Paddington'.

The band was better prepared for recording this time, with the orchestra already familiar with playing the band's material in the studio and on stage, including four songs which were earmarked for this new album: 'Mocking Bird', 'White Sails', 'Galadriel' and 'She Said'. 'Mocking Bird' had even been recorded at Abbey Road once already, on 18 May 1970, before the debut album had even been released, but both the band and Norman Smith considered that it needed further arrangement, and more effort had been expended on that in the meantime.

The resulting album, *Once Again*, is a far more assured and cohesive work, combining a very strong set of songs with some fine performances to create a classic, and an early high point of Barclay James Harvest's career. Some forty years later, Woolly Wolstenholme looked back with affection:

> On Once Again everything gelled in terms of songwriting. The album might be slightly juvenile and unsure of itself, but it has a sense of permanence about it, too. Material such as 'Mocking Bird' is very strong, and 'She Said' has

> that wonderfully evocative centre section. It all combines to make the album timeless in many ways.

The music press agreed, John Peel enthused, and although their verdict didn't translate into instant sales success, *Once Again* proved to be a slow burner, going on to qualify for a silver disc for £75,000 worth of sales in the UK. It is now regarded by many fans as one of the band's finest albums.

Sleeve Design

The original vinyl LP of *Once Again* came in a lavish gatefold sleeve, as was the norm for the early Harvest label releases. The design was by 'Latimer Reeves', Ian Latimer having been responsible for the band's debut album artwork, as well as designing album covers for the likes of Mark-Almond, UFO and Argent. The identity of 'Reeves' remains unknown. The *Once Again* sleeve was based on an enlarged section of the design for the debut album, giving the full butterfly effect only when opened out. The inside of the cover features a lot of white space and a cartoon butterfly, and maintains the group members' low profile (on album covers, at least) by omitting any mention of their names, whilst crediting just about everybody else involved! The American release on the Sire label has different artwork on the inside of the gatefold sleeve, using a negative image of a picture of the band by UK photographer and designer Terence Ibbott, well-known for his work on early Fleetwood Mac albums and many others.

'She Said' (Barclay James Harvest)

The opening track on *Once Again* was, along with 'Too Much On Your Plate', laid down on the first day of recording, 9 October 1970, and demonstrates just how far the band had come. 'She Said' is an absolute classic, soaring from the start with Woolly Wolstenholme's rising Mellotron note leading into John Lees' unmistakeable lead guitar riffs, the whole thing powered along by some expressive drumming from Mel Pritchard, married to Les Holroyd's nimble basslines. Although authorship is credited to John Lees on the sleeve and record labels, in fact, it was a true band effort. The piece's origins are to be found in two completely separate songs written by Les Holroyd; one called 'Miss Bailey', which included the 'She Said' verse, and the other being 'And I Will Always Love Her', which provided the chorus. At Woolly's instigation, the two songs were combined, with Woolly writing much of the arrangement and the link parts, and John coming up with the guitar solos. Woolly was responsible for the quiet central passage with its Elizabethan-style recorder solo, played by John, and Woolly also sang the lead vocal. His fondness for the song was reflected in the fact that it remained his favourite from the album decades later, and he continued to sing it live with John Lees' Barclay James Harvest right up to the very last concert he played with them, on 10 July 2010 in Porto, Portugal, before his untimely death in December of that year.

'Happy Old World' (Woolly Wolstenholme)

Woolly also sang lead on the next song, one of his own compositions, an environmental protest song long before there was widespread concern about the issue – as he put it, 'before there was greenness'! Some atmospheric, uneasy effects give way to gentle keyboard sounds for the verse, before the song bursts into life on the chorus. The contrast between the cheery, singalong chorus and the bleak message of the verses is stark, nowhere more so than when Woolly sings:

> My mind's not on this song I sing, my heart's not in the lines,
> Guess I'll go and kill myself, so would you kindly close the blinds

It's difficult to listen to in the knowledge of his suicide forty years later. Is it evidence that such sentiments had never been far away from his thoughts, or was he simply making a point for artistic effect? We may never know.

That Woolly certainly wasn't always in such a desolate frame of mind can be heard by listening to an alternative mix of the song which appeared in July 1973 on a version of the LP released to take advantage of the new-fangled quadraphonic surround sound system. An additional line towards the end of the coda of the song, 'as we travel through space', was spoken by Woolly as a jokey aside during recording, and was never intended to appear on the finished product! In fact, all of the 'extra' parts on the quad mix album were not overdubs, but parts of the original recording which had been removed or mixed well down during mixing and mastering for the normal stereo release. In some cases, such as some out of tune harmonies on 'Vanessa Simmons', it's not difficult to see why they were removed!

'Song For Dying' (Barclay James Harvest)

'The dawn's early light' in the opening line of this song is a phrase from 'The Star-Spangled Banner', and given the American national anthem's references to rockets, bombs and battles, a suitable introduction to John's anti-war polemic. Sung by Woolly, John's poignant lyric remembers not so much the dead, but the forgotten victims, the ones who are left behind:

> It's not for you we cry
> No, not for those who die
> It is only for their sons
> Forget the lives of others who are gone

Quiet piano chords set the scene before John's lead guitar and the Mellotron join in, with the whole piece underpinned by sensitive drumming and expressive bass. The version released on the *Once Again* album in 1971 builds to a crescendo before the Mellotron and busy bass parts fade away, but when research was underway for a 40th Anniversary CD edition, the original recording gathering dust in the vaults was found to have a two-minute instrumental coda which had been edited out for the original album. The lead guitar returns for an extended solo, ending up in a 'live in the studio' jam, and on the new edition, fans could finally hear the complete recording in its full glory. John Lees' Barclay James Harvest have also performed the song live in its unexpurgated version. Incidentally, the original working title for the song on the Abbey Road log sheets was 'Arrival'.

'Galadriel' (John Lees)

'Galadriel' is a delicate ballad which must rate as one of the most beautiful Barclay James Harvest songs ever recorded. The title comes from a character in Tolkien's *The Lord Of The Rings*, a recurring theme in BJH's early work (see Bombadil, and also 'Long Ships' from John's solo album, *A Major Fancy*). This is the song on which John played 'John Lennon's Guitar', the blond Epiphone which the great man can be seen playing in the famous film of The Beatles performing on the roof of the Apple Corps building in London's Savile Row on 30 January 1969. The guitar had been left in a cupboard at Abbey Road, and *Once Again*'s producer, Norman Smith, who had previously worked as sound engineer and later producer with The Beatles, fished it out to show it to the star-struck youngsters following in the fab four's footsteps. He even allowed John to use the instrument for the recording, and it is Lennon's guitar which you can hear on 'Galadriel'. Clearly, it inspired the other John, as the performance is both wistful and lovely. 'Oh, what it is to be young', indeed.

'Mocking Bird' (Barclay James Harvest)

Perhaps *the* definitive Barclay James Harvest classic, certainly for older fans from the band's home country, 'Mocking Bird' was first conceived in 1968 in a field up on Saddleworth Moor, when John had moved out of Preston House and into Sherbrooke Hall Farm, home of his new girlfriend's parents. Olwen, who would become John's wife, was the inspiration for the song and the first person to whom he played it. More than twenty-five years later, called as a witness in a court case brought by 'musical arranger' Robert Godfrey and hinging on who composed a number of early BJH songs, Olwen said, 'I remember John playing 'Mocking Bird' to me for the first time, just on the guitar on a sunny day outdoors.' Quizzed as to the unlikelihood of it including an orchestra arrangement at that point, Olwen quipped, 'I probably heard the orchestra in my head!'

The song would go on to become an evergreen prog-rock anthem, appearing in many guises in live performances and recordings throughout the next five decades, and still played live by both current incarnations of Barclay James Harvest. The song's commercial potential was clear, and a first professional recording of it was made at Abbey Road as early as 18 May 1970, before the release of the debut album. However, this version remained unreleased until many years later, when it appeared on the 40th Anniversary CD edition. Also included on that set was an extended non-orchestral version, demonstrating that the song was a *bona fide* classic in all its many guises. The team behind the Harvest label showed their faith in the song by releasing the full-length album track as a single not once but twice, albeit without reward. When the band left Harvest, label manager Nick Mobbs concluded a personal letter to John expressing his regret at their parting of the ways with the postscript, 'I still think Mocking Bird's a hit!'. Note for nature-lovers: there are seventeen species of mockingbird to be found around the world from the Americas to the Galapagos Islands, but not one is native to the U.K. Is it too fanciful to speculate whether that is why, in a bittersweet lyrical twist at the end of John's lyric, the mockingbird's song is no longer 'for you and me', but the bird is 'singing just for me'?

'Vanessa Simmons' (John Lees)

'Vanessa Simmons' is a simple acoustic ballad, a gentle, wistful piece sung from the world-weary perspective of an older man of twenty-three! Returning to the quadraphonic version of the album, the 'extra' parts were not always an unqualified success. This song illustrates perfectly why some harmonies were left off the original album, as the backing vocals on the 1973 surround sound LP are, on occasion, miles out of tune! For the true completist, there exists a 1974 pressing of the LP, issued only in Brazil, for which the Abbey Road sound engineers went back to the multi-tracks to remove the offending parts, creating a new mix which was also used on subsequent CD reissues of the quadraphonic album.

'Ball And Chain' (Barclay James Harvest)

Woolly's 'Ball And Chain' was a late contender for the album, owing its place to the exclusion of his preferred contribution, 'White Sails', due to the unsuitability of Robert Godfrey's orchestral arrangement for the latter. This angst-ridden rocker took its place, and a fine song it is, too. It was never performed live at the time because Woolly's voice couldn't cope night after night with the required vocal contortions, achieved in the studio with the aid of special effects (singing through a paper cup!). The haste in which it was recorded is underlined by the fact that when Woolly accidentally repeated one verse and omitted another, there wasn't enough studio time left to re-record it, so the verse which had been missed out was lost, and along with it, some of the thrust of the lyric:

> If I could live my whole life again
> I would not be on this prison train
> And I'd have no trouble from my ball and chain

Without the prison reference, the meaning of the song is more obscure, although it still provides a convincing allegory of the human condition.

'Lady Loves' (Barclay James Harvest)

The final track on the album was penned by John and sung by Woolly, and eases us out with the calm after the *Sturm und Drang* of 'Ball And Chain'. One curiosity of the recording is that it includes a musical contribution from a guest musician, a young tape-operator and engineer at Abbey Road by the name of Alan Parsons. Later to be a legendary figure in his own right, renowned not only as the engineer for Pink Floyd's *Dark Side Of The Moon*, but also for his own Alan Parsons Project, he later recalled being 'involved in probably three (Barclay James Harvest) albums all together. They were absolutely up my street; they were just the kind of music I really liked. I did a bit of engineering, a bit of tape op-ing. I even played the jaw's harp on a session for them once.' The twanging of the children's playground-favourite instrument contrasts oddly but pleasingly with the multi-tracked electric guitar of the coda and makes for a satisfyingly intriguing close to the album.

Related Songs:

'White Sails' (Woolly Wolstenholme)

Woolly's 'White Sails' tells of a yearning for escape, begging seafarers to take the writer along:

> Like beautiful birds, your ships with white sails
> Your romantic tales of uncharted trails
> Safe inside the wooden walls
> The white sails call to me

It had been performed live by the band in some of their 1969 and 1970 shows, including the orchestral concerts in June and July 1970, and it was planned to include it on the *Once Again* album. Unfortunately, the long, pseudo-classical arrangement, reminiscent of a piano concerto, written by Robert Godfrey and recorded with the orchestra at Abbey Road on 19 November 1970, was deemed completely unsuitable for a Barclay James Harvest album. The band never even got to record their parts, and the song was abandoned. It would be more than twenty years before the orchestral recording was unearthed from EMI's vaults when research was being undertaken for remastered CDs of the Harvest-era albums. Woolly oversaw the editing down of the opening section, which utilised Woolly's theme based on the chorus of the song, added some ambient 'sea noise', and it was added to the 2002 CD remaster of *Once Again* under the title, 'Introduction – White Sails (A Seascape)'.

'Too Much On Your Plate' (Barclay James Harvest)

Another regular in early BJH live sets was 'Too Much On Your Plate (It's Hard When Life Won't Do)', a rocker which shares a riff with 'Taking Some Time On', as well as manifesting influences from Cream and from Hendrix's version of 'Hey Joe'. It was the first song the band recorded at the Abbey Road album sessions, on 9 October 1970, but in the end, it was decided that it didn't quite fit with the more pastoral feel of the rest of the LP, and the recording was left to gather dust until it was released as a fan club exclusive flexidisc, given away with the December 1991 issue of club magazine *Nova Lepidoptera*. The song started life as a Woolly acoustic number based around the 'It's hard when life won't do...' section; then John added the chorus and heavy guitar riffs. A quite different mix was made by Norman Smith on 19 February 1971, possibly with a single release in mind, but again the plan was dropped, and the recording remained unreleased until it was included on the *Once Again* CD remaster in 2002.

Barclay James Harvest And Other Short Stories (1971)

Personnel:
John Lees: vocals, guitars
Les Holroyd: vocals, bass guitar, keyboards
Woolly Wolstenholme: vocals, keyboards
Mel Pritchard: drums and percussion
Orchestra manager and conductor: Martyn Ford
Orchestra leader: David Whiston
Arrangers: Toni Cooke and Martyn Ford
Recorded at EMI Studios, Abbey Road, July 1971 to October 1971
Producers: Wally Allen and Barclay James Harvest
Execute Producer: Norman Smith
Record Label: Harvest (UK), Sire (US)
UK release date: 5 November 1971

It seems crazy today that the band should record and release another album only months after *Once Again*, but the early seventies were another age when the careers of 'pop' musicians were expected to be short, and the pressure was on to capitalise on the critical acclaim and upwards momentum that Barclay James Harvest were enjoying – not to mention recouping some of the huge costs of playing live with an orchestra! Grandiose plans for a double album of one LP featuring the group on its own and the other with the group augmented by a full orchestra, and to record with the Boston Pops Orchestra in New York, were swiftly nixed by the record company in favour of the cheaper option of a single album to be made at Abbey Road. The band now had new management, and Martyn Ford had taken over managing the orchestra and writing arrangements, together with fellow French horn player, Toni Cooke, following the departure of Robert Godfrey in January 1971.

Although Norman Smith was credited as the album's 'Executive Producer', he was now much in demand as his *alter ego* Hurricane Smith, having scored a number 2 U.K. single with his own song, 'Don't Let It Die'. Having worked extensively with Harvest labelmates The Pretty Things, Smith had invited their bassist, Alan 'Wally' Waller, to become a staff producer at EMI, and now asked him to co-produce the new Barclay James Harvest album as his first major assignment. Adopting the alternative moniker 'Wally Allen' for his production role, Waller set to work. In theory, Smith would oversee the project, but in practice his direct involvement in the recording process was, said Wally:

> None at all. The emergence of Hurricane Smith as a career choice changed everything. I did, as a matter of courtesy, play him a couple of rough mixes – he tried to appear as interested as possible, but his world had been hit by a sea change, and his thoughts were no longer centred on other artists' musical output.

Those rough mixes are very likely the same ones which appeared on the *All Is Safely Gathered In* box set in 2006 – mono mixes of 'Medicine Man', 'Ursula' and 'Someone There You Know', with early vocal takes and before the orchestral parts were added. For the band, it was a challenge working with an inexperienced producer, but John was pleased enough with the results to work with Wally again on his solo album a year later:

> The noises were excellent, and the only bone I had with Wally was that he'd come in fresh so he did not know what we were trying to achieve. It wasn't until after we'd recorded Other Short Stories and he'd seen the different arrangements we'd got for stage that he realised what we were trying to do.

The recording sessions had to be fitted around the band's existing live commitments, including the legendary Weeley Festival, which took place on the August Bank Holiday weekend. Their busy schedule resulted in the studio time at Abbey Road being rather fragmented, spread over several sojourns, and running over into October. At last, the available studio time and budget simply ran out, and the album was declared complete. In the event, the rough edges and slight rawness of the finished product lend it a certain charm which some prefer to the more sumptuous feel of its illustrious predecessor, and in time it has come to be regarded by the band's many followers as a genuine classic in its own right.

Sleeve Design

For the first time in the band's career, the front cover, designed by Barry Honeyford, included photographs of the band members, and they were identified, at least by their first names, on the picture captions inside. The butterfly was still present, but only on the back of the sleeve this time. On the inside of the black, textured gatefold sleeve was a black and white group photo of the orchestra members and the band's managers, plus sleeve notes lampooning northern stereotypes, written by music journalist Roy Hollingworth – himself a northern(-ish) lad, born in Derby. The outdoor colour shots of the band members on the front and rear of the gatefold were taken by Hollingworth's *Melody Maker* colleague and sometime flatmate, Barry Wentzell.

'Medicine Man' (John Lees)

John explained the inspiration behind the song which, as a brand new composition, was one of the last to be recorded, in September 1971, but would become the classic opening track on the album:

> The song is based on the book Something Wicked This Way Comes by Ray Bradbury, which I read while flying to Germany for a holiday. After I'd finished the book, it so affected me that I wrote 'Medicine Man' immediately.

The title of the book is itself, of course, a quote from Shakespeare's Macbeth, and John would later use the same line in 'Lady Macbeth' from 1990's *Welcome To The Show* album. Bradbury is best known for his science fiction, and the book concerns a sinister travelling fair and a carousel which can make the riders of its flying horses grow younger or older – the calliope is the steam-powered mechanical organ which produces the carousel's music. Martyn Ford's original orchestral arrangement is suitably brooding, but the band members were not completely happy with their recording, rather to Ford's bemusement:

> I have to say that I think it sounds great. The weight of orchestration and the committed playing by the musicians greatly enhances this exciting and powerful piece, and I always remember it going down a storm at live gigs.

Notwithstanding, the band subsequently returned to 'Medicine Man' a number of times in the studio. Curiously, North American pressings of the album feature a completely different mix of the song, with more prominent drums and backing vocals (this version appears on the 2020 remastered editions of *Barclay James Harvest And Other Short Stories* issued by Esoteric Recordings), whilst a rockier, non-orchestral version of it was released on the B-side of the 1972 single, 'Thank You'. John finally got to meet the original book's author himself when they appeared on the same bill during BJH's short Stateside tour in 1976, and told him that he had written a song based on one of Bradbury's novels. The great man, who had almost certainly never heard of Barclay James Harvest, was, apparently, singularly unimpressed! Legions of fans thought otherwise and grew to love the song in its many and varied incarnations down the years, and it remains a favourite to this day in the live arena, where it is transformed into an amazing twelve-minute psychedelic prog-rock work out!

'Someone There You Know' (Barclay James Harvest)

Woolly's first contribution to *Other Short Stories* was written, like 'Ursula', about the end of Woolly's first great love affair, the loss of the girl to whom he was engaged after the eponymous Ursula went away to study English at University in Swansea. The gradual break-up had a profound effect on him, colouring the rest of his life, and was even the subject of one of the last songs which Woolly ever wrote, when he finally achieved 'Closure'. 'Someone There You Know' features Les on piano, whilst Woolly played the Mellotron parts. 'Someone There You Know' and 'Ursula' had already been aired in a Bob Harris BBC radio session, recorded on 29 June 1971 and first broadcast on 5 July, before the band began recording the album. The album version of 'Someone There You Know' sticks quite closely to that session arrangement, with Woolly's anguished vocals complemented by some gritty guitar licks from John. Incidentally, Woolly always insisted that the line in the chorus which follows 'your shadow's sinking low' was 'just like a stone', and not how it sounds, 'just like you're stoned'!

'Harry's Song' (John Lees)

When the band arrived at Abbey Road, they didn't have quite enough material prepared for a full album, so on 17 July 1971, the day before recording began in earnest on the album, John played a selection of his newest songs live in the studio for the other band members, and to bring Wally Allen up to speed. The first one he sang to them was 'Harry's Song', accompanied only by his acoustic guitar, and with incomplete lyrics, filled out with 'la la la's to give them an idea of the melody. Interestingly, on the demo, John segued the song into the opening bars of Woolly's 'Someone There You Know', perhaps with a thought to making the two songs run together on the album as a pair. Of the seven songs presented that day, his audience selected 'Harry's Song' as the one with the most potential, and the band began work immediately on a rocked-up version. Incidentally, the other songs which John demoed, but which didn't end up on the album, included two which would return in different guises in the future: 'Brave New World' and 'Hymn For A White Lady' – otherwise known as 'Hymn'! Once John had completed the lyrics of 'Harry's Song', the band returned to the recording studio in October, but by then time was running out. As Mel told *Zig Zag* magazine, 'One track, 'Harry's Song', was left unfinished because we just didn't have any time left to put on the piano, another guitar and all the vocals we wanted.' The recording may be a little rough around the edges, but even in its incomplete state, it works well, with the busy bass, lively drumming and edgy guitar complementing the enigmatic lyric well. So who was the titular Harry? The mystery was finally explained by John about twenty years later: 'It was written after the death of a much-loved family pet, a blue-fronted Amazon parrot, which gave us a lot of pleasure.' Well, if Monty Python could write about a dead parrot, why not Barclay James Harvest, too? Intriguingly, the closing line on the original demo was 'Young Harry's coming back to stay'. Stuffed, perhaps?

'Ursula (The Swansea Song)' (Barclay James Harvest)

Another brand new composition was Woolly's 'Ursula (The Swansea Song)', finished just before the band recorded the Bob Harris BBC session at the end of June, as Woolly explained:

> We came to the end of the session and were scratching around for some new numbers to record. I'd just written 'Ursula' and the arrangement hadn't really been thought out, but we let the tape machine roll and managed to put something down!

That barely-there but rather gorgeous piano-led session version of the song contrasts starkly with the finished recording on the album, where it is transformed into a kind of jolly sea-shanty, the music rather at odds with the poignancy of the lyrics. Woolly was heartbroken at the ending of his engagement to Ursula, admitting many years later that 'This one and 'Someone There You Know' were about the same thing, and were written at a particularly traumatic time in my life'. In 2012, Ursula herself recalled their time together and the separation:

> I got engaged to Woolly because he was the first mature man I'd dated, we both loved literature, words were important. He valued country life, he observed people, he had a sense of direction and he was so comfortable within my family. He had a sense of fun and humour; there was a playfulness in him. I loved that wry smile he had when his eyes would crinkle and his ginger moustache would twitch. I was at university and meeting people from other countries, other worlds. I was lost, out of place, falling, but at the same time felt there was a whole me and a whole world to discover. I broke off our relationship twice; I was becoming someone I didn't like in the way I was relating to Woolly; it had to end. I was pleased to hear after we'd broken up that he'd moved on quite quickly and met someone else.

The beautiful ending of the album version, with an F# major chord coming after an A major finish, was Woolly's attempt to link 'Ursula' with 'Little Lapwing' in a seamless segue, but to no avail, as on the finished pressings, a standard three-second gap was left between the tracks, completely neutralising the intended effect. This was finally remedied on a new stereo mix of the album for a 2020 deluxe remastered set issued by Esoteric Recordings.

'Little Lapwing' (Les Holroyd)

One of the first songs to be recorded for the album was 'Little Lapwing' – unique in the annals of Barclay James Harvest in that the music was all written and mostly performed by Les (acoustic guitars, twelve-string guitars, steel guitar, bass and piano, as well as the lead vocal!) but the lyrics were penned by John, returning to one of his favourite themes, birds, for inspiration. The orchestral coda was recorded later and edited on. Orchestra manager and arranger Martyn Ford remembered writing and recording for the album with great fondness, but this particular work with less enthusiasm:

> Having the opportunity to write for my own orchestra, and to record it at Abbey Road Studios was an amazing opportunity and one for which I am eternally grateful. 'Little Lapwing', on the other hand, sounds dated and weak to my ears, and I am mildly embarrassed by my naïve orchestration! It's certainly an album of extremes as far as both the material and the production values are concerned. These were exciting times, and I only wish we could do it all over again! Happy Days!

'Song With No Meaning' (Les Holroyd)

This is another quintessentially English pastoral song with the music composed by Les, with some assistance from his girlfriend Christine and from Mel, with the lyrics. It's a charming, ethereal piece, perfectly capturing the lazy, hazy days of a long-forgotten summer, reminiscing wistfully about a departed lover – a recurring theme on this album! Two phrases in the lyrics, describing 'A silhouette against the sky' and how 'The seconds they dripped right on by, and slowly filled the day' bring to mind lines in the later compositions 'Paper

Wings' and 'Negative Earth', where virtually all of the lyrics were written by Mel, so it seems a fair bet that this stanza came from his pen. In similar fashion to 'Little Lapwing', Les played nearly all the guitars on 'Song With No Meaning', with the exception of some twelve-string courtesy of Woolly.

'Blue John's Blues' (John Lees)

Written perhaps more in sorrow than in anger, John's gritty 'Blue John's Blues' was recorded on the same day as 'Song With No Meaning'. The lyrics include an acerbic sideswipe at the music business and the position in which the band found themselves at the time, while also evoking happier, albeit still melancholic, memories of female company. 'Joe Crow' was the abbreviation by which their former manager, John Crowther, was known. The deceptively simple opening piano chords give way to a rocking chorus and the whole thing ends in a gloriously chaotic boogie and some lovely twin-tracked lead guitar phrases.

'The Poet' (Woolly Wolstenholme)

The final song to be recorded was 'The Poet', an introspective piece penned by Woolly in the formative days of the band, as he later told the band's fan club magazine:

> The song was written in 1967, and is really having a go at the self-importance of 'the artist' – that kind of 'sit next to me and listen but don't touch or criticise' attitude.

A decision was made to link 'The Poet' with 'After the Day', so Toni Cooke and Martyn Ford went away and wove an orchestral arrangement which became one of the defining moments of the completed LP. A sweet variation on the melody of 'The Poet' gradually morphs into something much darker and more sinister, brooding cellos building to a crescendo which momentarily hangs in mid-air until John's guitar and the rest of the band come crashing in with 'After the Day'. Martyn was delighted with the result:

> Revisiting the album decades later, it is remarkable how fresh some of it sounds. There was a very talented musician and horn player at the Academy, a friend of mine called Toni Cooke, and I asked her to write [the arrangement for] 'The Poet' and I think I did 'After The Day'. We kind of did it between us, and I was a bit twitchy about it! It is greatly enhanced by Toni Cooke's beautiful French horn playing, and Toni wrote the amazing orchestral link between 'The Poet' and 'After the Day'.

It's a masterpiece of arrangement, and has latterly been recreated in John Lees' Barclay James Harvest live shows, first by Woolly, then on later tours by Jez Smith, with John singing 'The Poet' in numerous shows as a tribute to Woolly, who finally lost his battle with depression in 2010.

'After The Day' (John Lees)

John's vision of Armageddon closes the album with a bang - literally! The references in the lyric to a stained-glass window ('one great wall of coloured parts') and 'the multi-coloured cross left standing through it all' add religious overtones to the apocalyptic feel of the song, which was a live favourite for many years, particularly in the days of the band's concerts with the orchestra, and made a triumphant return to the live arena in the twenty-first century, when it was reintroduced into concert settings first by Woolly and his band Mæstoso, then by Woolly and John together in John Lees' Barclay James Harvest.

The superb orchestration has already been covered in the entry for 'The Poet' above, but what's less well-known is that Wally Allen also made a musical contribution to 'After The Day':

> I had an idea for the harmony on 'After The Day'. I sang it to them, and they liked it. I think we tried both Woolly and Les on the part, but it wasn't sounding right. Finally, I think it was Woolly who said 'I think you'd better sing it, Wal, it suits your underground voice.' I'm not quite sure what an underground voice is or was, but anyway, when it came to mixing the track I kept it well to the rear!

Modest to a fault, but however the band, orchestra and production team arrived at the finished result, it remains – to these ears – not only one of the finest tracks that Barclay James Harvest ever recorded, but also a contender for a hitherto neglected, but surely overdue, 'best fusion of rock and classical music' award!

Related Songs:

'Brave New World' (Lees/Wolstenholme)

Included on remastered versions of *And Other Short Stories* was this John Lees song, which was one of the seven songs demoed by him at Abbey Road in July 1971. Tracing a life from the innocence of childhood to despair by early adulthood, all the way through to an empty world-weariness in old age, it's a stunning achievement from a writer who was only twenty-four when he composed it. All the more surprising, then, that its merits weren't recognised at the time, and that the song lay undiscovered until Woolly suggested that he and John revisit it as part of their *Nexus – Barclay James Harvest Through The Eyes Of John Lees* project. For that 1998 recording, Woolly re-wrote the chorus, because:

> The original 1971 version, demoed at Abbey Road on acoustic guitar, showed its folk roots and had a chorus that seemed inappropriate to its disillusioned message. A more contemporary salsa feel and references to 'Galadriel' and 'Brother Thrush' continue in the same vein.

The recording of the 1971 demo finally gained an official release in 1999 on a fan club exclusive CD EP called *The Origin Of Pieces*, showcasing early recordings of some songs from the *Nexus* album.

Baby James Harvest (1972)

Personnel:
John Lees: vocals, guitars
Les Holroyd: vocals, bass guitar, keyboards
Woolly Wolstenholme: vocals, keyboards, bells and Tam Tam
Mel Pritchard: drums and percussion
Barclay James Harvest Symphony Orchestra, conductor: Martyn Ford
Orchestra leader: Alan Travers
Arrangers: Brian Day ('Delph Town Morn'), Martyn Ford and John Bell ('Moonwater')
Recorded at Strawberry Studios, Stockport and EMI Studios, Abbey Road, September 1972
Producers: Barclay James Harvest
Engineers: Peter Tattersall (Strawberry), Mike Sheady and Kete Go (Abbey Road)
Record Label: Harvest
UK release date: 10 November 1972

In contemporary interviews, the band members had been talking about plans for a lavish double album set with the working title *Four Winds*, which might feature one side of each of the individual musicians' ideas, but reality soon set in. What with the band's gruelling live workload, which left little time for writing, and the tightening of record company purse strings in the face of the band's rapidly mounting debts, such grandiose projects were soon scaled down. Most of the recording would take place in Stockport, at Strawberry Studios, co-owned by Peter Tattersall and 10cc's Eric Stewart, thus keeping costs down. Only the pieces which would require an orchestra would be done at Abbey Road – which in the event, meant only one composition: Woolly's 'Moonwater'. This resulted in what more than one of the band members later described as a 'schizophrenic album', particularly when technical issues with the recording of 'Moonwater' necessitated Woolly spending even more time in London, forcing the other three to get on with recording at Strawberry in his absence.

The end result was that three of *Baby James Harvest*'s six songs didn't include any contributions at all from Woolly, whilst John, Les and Mel didn't play or sing on 'Moonwater' at all, leaving only two songs on which all four members of the band were featured.

In spite of this unintended foretaste of a future when Barclay James Harvest would become a trio, and Woolly a solo artist, it's not a bad album – just a little weaker than its illustrious predecessors from the previous year, which had set the bar impossibly high. It certainly wasn't as bad as John's gloomy assessment in later years, when he said, 'We should have wiped the tapes', and described the LP as 'ashtray material'! Whilst never likely to rank highly in polls of fans' favourite Barclay James Harvest albums, it still has its staunch supporters. 'Summer Soldier' alone is a genuine BJH classic, and there is much to enjoy elsewhere on the record. However, the album seems a little disjointed and unsure of what it wants to be, ranging from folk and unpretentious rock and roll to brass band and classical music. It has a *fin de siècle* feeling about it, and would, indeed, prove to be the last album which Barclay James Harvest recorded for the Harvest label.

Sleeve Design

The 'baby' theme was the idea of Ian Cassie, a former social secretary at the Manchester College of Commerce who had, together with Dave Crowe, run The White Agency, dedicated to artist concert bookings, and had now taken over management duties from John Crowther. The front cover was created by Julian Cottrell, an up and coming photographer working out of his own studio in New Burlington Street in London's West End. Cottrell had worked as an assistant to luminaries like Lester Bookbinder and Richard Avedon, and the film director David Puttnam (*Chariots Of Fire* et al.) was once his photographic agent! Almost forty years on, in March 2010, Cottrell still remembered his BJH commission:

> I very much enjoyed making the cover photograph for the album Baby James Harvest. It was actually my daughter Boo in the flower pot! She is now 41!! I am still a working photographer – I went into film commercials for twenty years and have only in the last ten years been taking photographs again, which was always my first love.

The album title followed on from the photograph, as well as being a jokey reference to James Taylor's classic album from 1970, *Sweet Baby James*. The Harvest label's diminishing budget is evident in the fact that an expensive gatefold was eschewed in favour of a single sleeve, although original copies also included an inner sleeve with the band's trademark butterfly prominent on one side and a list of all the performers on each song on the other.

'Crazy (Over You)' (Les Holroyd)

Les gets us underway with his bass leading into a trademark Lees guitar riff and a mid-paced, catchy love song which never quite hits the heights, but is a pleasant enough opener. Les played organ and Mellotron as well as the bass and taking the lead vocal, whilst Woolly contributed the piano part.

'Delph Town Morn' (John Lees)

Woolly is entirely absent from John's first contribution to the album, which is also unusual in that it features not only John, Les and Mel but also a thirteen-piece brass section from the Syd Lawrence Orchestra on an arrangement written and conducted by Brian Day. Barry Thompson, Bill Newton, Norman Brown, Nat Whitworth and George Watts played alto, tenor and baritone saxes; Dave Browning, Lennie Moakes, Don Banks and Brom Harvey appeared on trumpet, together with trombonists Frank Dixon, Miff King, Frank Brierley and Austin Gleave. Subsequently, Syd's son, Martin Lawrence, would also be involved with BJH as a sound engineer and producer, having first appeared on 1976's *Octoberon* album in a singing capacity! The Delph Town of the title is the Saddleworth village where John was living at the time, and 'Chris's son' in the first line of the lyrics is actually Les Holroyd! The song, a minor neglected gem in the band's catalogue, finally received a belated live airing when it was performed by John Lees' Barclay James Harvest as part of an acoustic medley during a 50th-anniversary concert at the Royal Northern College of Music in Manchester in May 2018, to the delight of long-time aficionados.

'Summer Soldier' (John Lees)

The epic which closed side one of the original LP was inspired by a subject which would preoccupy John over the years: the futility of violence and a plea for peace. The lyrics, touching on bombers and soldiers being stoned, clearly refer to The Troubles in Northern Ireland, which were much in the news in the immediate aftermath of 'Bloody Sunday'. This was a tragic event on 30 January 1972, when more than a dozen unarmed protesters against internment were shot dead by the British Army in Derry. Sadly, the theme is universal. The inner sleeve of the LP gives 'Special thanks to Woolly for arrangement at the end', which rather bemused the man himself, who considered that the credit made it sound as though he wasn't actually a member of the band, even though he actually played some of the organ and Mellotron parts on the recording. It is easy to imagine that tensions were running a little high with his absence for the most part from the studio and the rushed way in which the album was put together.

'Thank You' (Les Holroyd)

Incorrectly credited to Les on the LP, 'Thank You' is actually a John Lees song and was a late addition to the line-up, throwing together a fine guitar riff with a musical credits list, which decodes as follows:

Dixie (Kidd) – the owner of the Dandelion music shop in Huddersfield, from whom the band bought some instruments, including one of John's Fender Stratocasters
Pete (Tattersall) – the owner and manager of Inter-City Sound and Strawberry Studios
Teddy (Meyers) – head of EMI Switzerland
Eddie (Buckley) – a member of the road crew
Ollie (Olwen Lees) – John's wife
Chris (Christine) – Les's girlfriend, later wife
Janet (Pritchard) – then Mel's wife
Snibbley – Ian Southerington, sound engineer
Heather (Crowe) – Dave Crowe's wife
Georgie – Middle name of Dave Crowe, one of the band's managers at the time
The waterfall – Dave and Heather's baby boy
Cassie – Ian Cassie, the band's other manager

Nicky (Mobbs) – head of Harvest Records
Ricky (Dixon) – of Kennedy Street Enterprises, the band's concert agents
Eric (Stewart) – a member of Hotlegs and 10cc and partner in Strawberry Studios
Kev (Godley) & Lol (Creme) – of Hotlegs and 10cc
Billy Bean's Machine – Kev and Lol's 'gizmo' effects machine for electric guitars.

This was an early 'trio' recording, with no input from Woolly, and was also released as a single on 20 October 1972 as a trailer for the album, backed with a new recording of 'Medicine Man'.

'One Hundred Thousand Smiles Out' (Les Holroyd)

Les's rather lovely song is about the isolation of an astronaut lost in space, a theme to which he would subsequently return in 'Negative Earth'. The 'space race' was a staple of the news media after the first manned expedition to the moon in 1969, and that interest was reflected in many other songs from that period on the same subject, famously including David Bowie's 'Space Oddity' and Elton John's 'Rocket Man'. At more than six minutes long, the recording perhaps outstays its welcome a little with an extremely long fade-out, reflecting the paucity of new material the band had ready for the album. Les again played the piano in Woolly's absence.

'Moonwater (*Poco Adagio*)' (Woolly Wolstenholme)

In the meantime, Woolly was at Abbey Road in London, working on his own epic. The idea was to record the orchestral pieces, then take the tapes up to Stockport for him and the rest of the band to record their parts. However, when Woolly arrived, the tapes wouldn't play properly, with extraneous noises on some tracks ruining the recording, so he had to get back on the train to London and do them again – to no avail, as the problem persisted, and a compromise solution of mixing down the affected tracks had to be utilised. Time was so short that the other three couldn't wait for him, so much of the recording of the rest of the album went ahead without him, whilst 'Moonwater' ended up with no contributions from the other three band members. Woolly described the piece as his 'attempt to bridge the gap between Radios One and Three', and dedicated it to Gustav Mahler, whose work had a big influence on him; 'the Countess' was a real Polish countess who worked for a London publishing company, and the 'additional material' by Les was actually a Mellotron part taken from 'Eden Unobtainable', an early song which wouldn't get an official release for almost twenty years. And *poco adagio*? A little bit faster than the 'slow and stately' *adagio*. Fast forward to 2002, when a remastered CD of *Baby James Harvest* was scheduled for release, and Woolly decided to check the multi-tracks to see whether the noise which had spoilt the original could be removed. To his astonishment, there was no trace of it, and he and veteran engineer Peter Mew completed the 2002 remix with all of Woolly's original arrangement intact before the explanation dawned: the machine they were using at Abbey Road was, in all likelihood, the very same one on which the original recording had been made thirty years before, and with the same engineer ... The tape machine at Strawberry Studios back in 1972 must have been set up differently, and thus incapable of replaying the tapes correctly.

Related Songs:

'I'm Over You' (John Lees)

Under pressure from EMI after the relative commercial failure of previous singles, BJH embarked on a series of what John later described as disastrous attempts to come up with a hit single during 1972. This first effort, released on the Harvest label on 28 April, was a pleasant love song, with a great deal of charm, but didn't set the charts alight.

'Child of Man' (John Lees)

The B-side of 'I'm Over You' was, in many ways, more interesting than the more commercial A-side, and introduced a religious theme which would be a recurring element in John's songs over the years. An alternative version was recorded for Bob Harris's BBC Radio show shortly before the single's release and is to be found on remastered CDs of *Baby James Harvest*. The BBC recording has slightly different lyrics, with John substituting 'The son of God knelt down to pray' for the single version's 'The child of man knelt down to pray', making the Christian reference more explicit.

'Breathless' (Terry Bull) [as 'Bombadil']

Instructed to pursue that elusive hit, the band, collective tongue firmly in cheek, came up with this piece of bubblegum – a bit of instrumental foolery in a pastiche of contemporary glam rock, typified by the likes of Chicory Tip in the charts. Unsurprisingly, when Harvest actually wanted to release it as a single, the decision was made to do so under an alias, to preserve the band's progressive credentials! Thus, it appeared under the band name Bombadil, and promptly disappeared without trace! In the same spirit of anonymity, the writer of the A-side (for which the blame should mostly have been laid at the door of Woolly and John) was credited, appropriately enough, as Terry Bull!

'When The City Sleeps' (Lester Forest) [as 'Bombadil']

For reassurance, the traditional BJH fan had to turn to the B-side to find this Woolly song about walking through deserted city streets in the small hours. It's largely a solo recording, with Woolly responsible for all of the keyboards and vocals, plus Eric Stewart of 10cc on bass guitar and Mel Pritchard on tambourine. It, too, was credited to Bombadil for the single, with the writer purporting to be one Lester Forest. This is possibly not unconnected with the fact that one of the band's regular motorway services stops on their travels was at Leicester Forest ...

'Rock and Roll Woman' (Les Holroyd)

A final push by EMI for a hit single led to what would become the band's last recording for Harvest, made in early 1972 and annotated with the hopeful working title 'Top Pop' on the Abbey Road log sheet. Les, who was planning to record a solo album at the time, told the *New Musical Express* how the song came about:

> The new single started off as just a guitar phrase which I was going to develop into a song for my album. But we were in the studio and after we started kicking it around, we thought it might make a good single.

By the time it was mixed, though, even Les was unsure of its merits:

> Once you start adding and mixing, you go through it forty or fifty times and you come out with a product you don't know. You just don't know how good it is any more.

Les's reservations were well-founded, as the clichéd lyrics and rather tired-sounding performance made the single, released on 4 May 1973, a slightly pedestrian ending to their illustrious sojourn on the Harvest label.

'The Joker' (Holroyd/Lees)

In fact, the B-side of 'Rock And Roll Woman', a fine writing collaboration between Holroyd and Lees entitled 'The Joker', is a much stronger song. The lyrics concern man's inhumanity to man, ending with the hopeful observation that 'it's not too late to see we're all the same'. Musically, the opening guitar riff bears some similarity to the introduction of 'Capricorn' many years later, and the wonderful crescendo produced by the rising backing vocals adds a very original touch.

Everyone Is Everybody Else (1974)

Personnel:
John Lees: vocals, lead guitar, acoustic guitar
Les Holroyd: vocals, bass guitar, acoustic guitar, rhythm guitar ('picked' guitar on 'Poor Boy Blues' and 'Mill Boys')
Woolly Wolstenholme: vocals, keyboards
Mel Pritchard: drums and percussion
Recorded at Olympic Studios, London, March to April 1974; mixed/mastered at Trident Studios, London
Producer: Rodger Bain
Engineers: Rufus Cartwright (Olympic), Ted Sharp (Trident)
Record Label: Polydor
UK release date: 14 June 1974

Without a recording contract, in debt and now managerless, too, having dispensed with the services of Ian Cassie and Dave Crowe, the future looked bleak for Barclay James Harvest. John asked his friend Eric Stewart for advice, and he recommended that BJH approach 10cc's manager, Harvey Lisberg, the Manchester-based impresario who had discovered Herman's Hermits, Andrew Lloyd Webber and Tim Rice and many more. In December 1973 Lisberg secured a new contract for Barclay James Harvest with Polydor Records, to take effect from January 1974, in return for taking on the band's management and publishing. The deal marked a turning point for BJH, freeing them from their debts to EMI, and in March 1974 they set to work on a new studio album at Olympic Studios in Barnes, South-West London, the birthplace of many classic recordings by the likes of The Who and Led Zeppelin – and Procol Harum's 'A Whiter Shade Of Pale'.

John told *Sounds* music paper eighteen months later: 'The first Polydor album was a really good feel. It was completely fresh, and we'd got a new producer. We went in feeling terrific and there were people at Polydor, like Hedley Leighton and Wayne Bickerton, who really believed in us'.

The new producer was the man responsible for Black Sabbath's first three albums, Rodger Bain, and whilst a heavy rock specialist wasn't the obvious choice for BJH, Bain's production gave the album a harder edge, shorn of their earlier work's lavish orchestral arrangements, now abandoned because of the prohibitive costs. A combination of very strong material, the band's determination to make a new start and the producer's firm guiding hand resulted in an album which successfully captured their more powerful live sound, and is widely regarded as one of the finest in the Barclay James Harvest canon. Although the album didn't chart, it was generally well-received at the time – most notably by Radio One DJ John Peel, who commented on air that when he received a new album he was in the habit of making marks next to each song he considered worthy of airplay on his show, and that in the case of *Everyone Is Everybody Else*, found that he had marked every track! The band's fans regard it as a classic, and the high esteem in which it is still held to this day was demonstrated in October 2018, when, as part of the inaugural U.K. National Album Day, John Lees' Barclay James Harvest performed *Everyone Is Everybody Else* in its entirety for the first and only time to a rapturous sell-out crowd at London's Islington Assembly Hall.

Sleeve Design

A straightforward, if rather unimaginative, choice of cover art, consisting simply of a photo of the band taken on their home territory by Alex Agor, with another shot from the same session, of them peering out through the broken windows of a derelict farmhouse, on the reverse of the single sleeve. Signalling another break with the EMI-era, the trademark butterfly was nowhere to be seen, replaced by a new circular BJH logo. The original LP came with a plain white inner sleeve and no lyrics, and first pressings have a matt sleeve with the band photo on the back of the cover in colour on a dark green background, whilst later copies firstly used glossy card and then a black and white back. Art direction was by Vincent McEvoy, a Polydor in-house designer whose work can also be seen on contemporary album covers by artists including Jimi Hendrix, Cream and Rare Bird.

'Child Of The Universe' (John Lees)

The cracking first track on the album was actually an older song which had previously been rejected for BJH, and had been recorded by John in 1972 as part of a solo album for the Harvest label. However, when the band were dropped by EMI, that album was shelved, and having heard the solo recording, the other members of the band and the producer decided that 'Child Of The Universe' should be revisited. The song, a lament for the violent ways of man, with references to the Vietnam War and civil unrest in Northern Ireland, rapidly established itself as a timeless BJH classic, which became a staple on Radio Caroline and in the group's live shows. John dedicated this recording to the memories of John Kershaw, John Crowther and Gerald Doyle – Kershaw and Doyle were relatives of John's, whilst John Crowther, the band's first manager, died tragically young during a routine dental operation, still in his twenties. The band members weren't entirely satisfied with their recording of 'Child Of The Universe', so when the American arm of Polydor wanted to release the song as a single to promote the album, the decision was made to re-record it at Polydor Studios in Central London with Rodger Bain on 5 January 1975. Still unsure about the results, they made another attempt just over a week later on 13 January at Advision Studios, less than a mile away, and yet a third on 21 February, again at Advision. Ironically, after all that effort, Bain chose the first January recording for the single, which was duly released Stateside in April 1975, even though John, at least, disagreed with Rodger's choice:

> It might have worked if Rodger hadn't been so into heavy rock. The stumbling block was 'Child Of The Universe', which we must have recorded three times as a single for the States, and the final cut was terrible. Nothing against Rodger, but it just didn't happen.

All three of the re-recordings can be found on remastered CDs of *Everyone Is Everybody Else* and *Time Honoured Ghosts.* In July 1977 John's solo album, *A Major Fancy*, belatedly got a release on the Harvest label, and an edited version of the 1972 recording of 'Child Of The Universe' was issued as a single to promote it.

'Negative Earth' (Les Holroyd/Mel Pritchard)

A very underrated song in the BJH catalogue, possibly because of its unusual, syncopated rhythm and sparse arrangement. The inspiration was the near-disastrous Apollo 13 space mission in April 1970, when an explosion forced the astronauts to use the lunar module Aquarius as a 'life raft' to return to Earth. Les wrote the music but was struggling for lyrics, and Mel stepped into the breach:

> Les had got this thing that I couldn't get out of my head, and I wrote everything except 'For fifty-five days …'. It struck a chord with me, I just thought about the isolation of this guy.

Mel was a great admirer of Simon and Garfunkel, and his lyrics for 'Negative Earth', as well as wittily referencing the song's structure ('here in syncopated time, while my tangled web of rhyme, dangles aimlessly …') also echo Simon's earlier song, 'The Dangling Conversation'. 'Negative Earth' also appeared on a free flexidisc single (backed with Rare Bird's 'Diamonds') which was given away with *Sounds* as a promotional tool for the U.K. tour undertaken by both bands in May and June of 1974. A different recording of the song was broadcast as part of a Bob Harris BBC radio session in September 1974, and can be found on the *After The Day - The Radio Broadcasts 1974-1976* double CD issued in 2008.

'Paper Wings' (Les Holroyd/Mel Pritchard)

Another Holroyd/Pritchard collaboration, with Les composing the music and Mel the words:

> I wrote all the lyrics to 'Paper Wings'. I was up the Eiffel Tower and I'm not gifted with a head for heights, so I got to the first stage. The rest of the guys went up and I came down, and there's a plaque at the bottom and this dent in the floor – it's like 'Suicide', was he pushed or did he jump? It was basically that he was 'a broken man without a dream' because if he jumped and he couldn't fly it was a broken dream, or if somebody pushed him then it's still a vision that finished up as a bump in the floor. I'd like to do more. I like lyrics, but with such good lyricists as we've got it's very hard.

'Paper Wings', with its powerful instrumental second half driven along by Mel's powerhouse drumming, proved another very popular live number and a slightly different version was also recorded, along with three other tracks from this album, for a John Peel BBC session in August 1974. That version also appears on the *After The Day - The Radio Broadcasts 1974-1976* compilation.

'The Great 1974 Mining Disaster' (John Lees)

'The Great 1974 Mining Disaster' was John's riposte to a suggestion from within the band that they should pursue a more commercial sound, like that of The Bee Gees. John's answer was to deconstruct the Brothers Gibb's 1967 hit, 'New York Mining Disaster 1941' and re-write it, changing both melody and lyrics to turn the song into a political comment on the 1974 UK miners' strike which finally brought down the Conservative government of the day. Subtle alterations to the original lyrics such as changing 'don't go talking too loud, you'll cause a landslide' into 'all you have to do is smile to cause a landslide' are combined with veiled references to contemporary political and musical figures. 'A sailor oh so gay' was Ted Heath, a keen yachtsman who captained Britain's winning team for the Admiral's Cup in 1971 during his term as Prime Minister, and who was widely rumoured to be gay. 'Mister Groan' was miners' leader Joe Gormley, and John's lyrics also allude to two songs by David Bowie ('The Man Who Sold The World' and 'Space Oddity', about 'a major out in space').

'Crazy City' (Les Holroyd)

The second side of the LP kicked off in fine style with one of the best songs ever penned by Les. The message of 'Crazy City' disparages city dwelling in favour of country living, and was apparently written about London, although it could equally apply to the frenetic pace of life in any big city. It's clear that the arrangement was a true band effort, with John's opening riff and double-tracked lead guitar parts complemented by Woolly's subtle keyboard embellishments and Mel's fine drumming. The excellent three-part harmonies sung by John, Les and Woolly in the middle reveal a taste for the vocal talents of Crosby, Stills, Nash and Young, perennial favourites of the members of Barclay James Harvest, particularly Les. Perhaps surprisingly, the song was never released as a single, although it was used as the B-side of 'Child Of The Universe' when that came out in the U.S.A. and France and as the flip side of 'Poor Boy Blues' in the U.K. and Germany. An alternative recording was also broadcast as part of the 1974 John Peel session.

'See Me See You' (John Lees)

Some lachrymose Harrison-esque guitar introduces 'See Me, See You', a John Lees composition written on the band's return from their ill-advised tour of South Africa in the autumn of 1972. The track is notable for some stream of consciousness word-play in the lyrics which lift it out of the ordinary run of love songs. The repeated twin-guitar motif is overlaid with the solo as John experiments with new textures, and there's a cheeky 'Hey Jude' added to the end of the chorus. The song was never performed live by Barclay James Harvest, but it finally made its concert debut forty-four years after its first release, when John Lees' Barclay James Harvest performed it at the Milton Keynes Stables and Islington Assembly Hall during their 2018 U.K. tour.

'Poor Boy Blues' (Les Holroyd)

And now we come to what many fans regard as the album's crowning glory, the 'holy trilogy', as John Lees' Barclay James Harvest flippantly dubbed it when they performed it live in later years: a triumvirate of songs woven together to form a mini-suite. The first of the three, 'Poor Boy Blues', is a lilting Les Holroyd song with a country-ish feel, something which Les was on record as saying that he wanted to explore in a solo album, planned for the early seventies but never recorded. Having written a song with some overlap in the subject matter, John set about combining this song and his own 'Mill Boys', to great effect. The verse of 'Mill Boys' becomes an instrumental middle eight in 'Poor Boy Blues', whilst the chorus of 'Poor Boy Blues' is turned into the instrumental middle eight for 'Mill Boys'. The whole section is topped and tailed by Les's almost *a capella* intro to 'Poor Boy Blues', which returns as a coda to 'Mill Boys'. 'Poor Boy Blues' was released as a single in the U.K. and Germany three weeks before the appearance of *Everyone Is Everybody Else*, backed with 'Crazy City'.

'Mill Boys' (John Lees)

Not for the first time (*cf.* 'Delph Town Morn'), John turned to the area where he grew up for inspiration, but in this case, he was thinking of historic times. The subject of the song is specifically the Lancashire cotton mining industries, with its mentions of mules spinning (the spinning mule was a machine for turning cotton fibres into yarn) and 'black-faced lifers' (coal miners). Some of the references are very specific to the area, name-checking places such as Tandle Hills (sung as 'Tangle 'ills' in keeping with the local pronunciation) and Shaw Road, a street in nearby Royton, a suburb of Oldham in the present-day metropolitan county of Greater Manchester. The reprise of 'Poor Boy Blues' at the end rounds things off nicely, and leads us straight into:

'For No One' (John Lees)

'For No One', crashing in with all guitars, Mellotron, drums and bass blazing, is a superb way to end the album. We're taken back to the opening theme of the album with another hard-hitting anti-war song from the pen of John Lees, a powerful statement in which you can hear the anger as he tells us to 'lay down your pistols and your rifles' and then 'lay down your bullshit', before concluding 'God alone knows how we will survive'. The version that the band played in concert, as captured on the *Barclay James Harvest Live* album from later that same year, was even more impressive, building up to an exquisite and dramatic ending, as opposed to the studio version, which fades out in the middle of a rather good wah-wah guitar solo. The song has been regularly included in live concerts down the ensuing years, and a John Peel session studio recording replicates the live ending. A fabulous way to end a fine album, which has a very special place in many fans' affections.

Related Songs:

'Mæstoso (A Hymn in the Roof of the World)' (Woolly Wolstenholme)

Everyone Is Everybody Else was the first Barclay James Harvest album not to include any compositions by Woolly Wolstenholme, but it wasn't planned to be that way. His 'magnum opus', as he described it, had already been in gestation for some time; it was finally tabled for inclusion on this album and was duly recorded at Olympic Studios in the spring of 1974 during the album sessions. However, Rodger Bain decided that it was at odds with the rest of the songs on the album, and as producer he had the final say. To Woolly's dismay, the recording was unceremoniously ditched. The song's lyrics imagine a chance meeting between American and Russian mountaineers at the summit of Mount Everest, where Nepal and Tibet meet, and the music and bombastic arrangement is as heroic as the theme. In Woolly's own words, 'The original concept of the pointlessness of national endeavour and the ultimate triumph of humanity now sounds naïve and idealistic – but it fits the music!'

Woolly did re-record the piece as the title track of his 1980 solo album, *Mæstoso*, but this shorter version, with Mel's drumming to the forefront, didn't get a release until it was included on the 1996 BJH rarities compilation, *Endless Dream*, and was finally restored to its rightful place on remastered editions of *Everyone Is Everybody Else*.

Time Honoured Ghosts (1975)

Personnel:
John Lees: electric and acoustic guitars, vocals
Les Holroyd: bass and acoustic guitars, vocals
Woolly Wolstenholme: keyboards, vocals
Mel Pritchard: percussion
Recorded at His Master's Wheels studio, San Francisco, May to July 1975
Producer: Elliot Mazer
Engineers: Jeremy Zatkin, Elliot Mazer (recording), George Horn, Phil Brown (mastering)
Record Label: Polydor
UK release date: October 1975
Highest chart places: UK: 32, The Netherlands: 34

During the last few months of 1974, the band spent some time in between gigs at Strawberry Studios, recording demos for their next album. However, plans to record a new studio album at the end of 1974 or in the early weeks of 1975 were revised because of the unexpected success of *Barclay James Harvest Live*, a double LP released in November 1974, which became their first Top 40 album, and because of the band's continuing tour commitments. Happily, the timing coincided with the availability of producer Elliot Mazer, who had already expressed an interest in the band. Known principally for his work with Neil Young on classic albums such as *Harvest*, he had seen the Barclays performing at the Royal Festival Hall in 1973, and felt that 'good songs make good records, and the skills of Barclay James Harvest match up to any of the great artists.' The band flew out to San Francisco at the end of April to begin work at Mazer's own His Master's Wheels studio. The album took two months to record, and whilst John, Les and Mel were fans of American acts like The Eagles and Poco, and were happy with Mazer's American West Coast sensibilities, Woolly had mixed feelings:

> Some of the band thought it might be some kind of extra injection of energy or whatever if we went over to the States and made an album there. So we did that, and I wasn't really happy with it. Neil Young-type laid back and spaced out was the order of the day, and you felt a bit like that, I must confess, but we weren't producing English music, so it seemed a bit of a waste of having a natural resource and then trying to do something else with it. I had trouble getting my ideas across to Elliot Mazer, who didn't really understand the British way of thinking.

In spite of Woolly's misgivings, the album, released in October 1975, built on the sales of the live album, climbing to number 32 in the U.K. album chart and going silver within six weeks. Even the reviews, whilst not all favourable, were considerably better than the band had received for some years. A number of radio and television appearances further enhanced the band's reputation, notably a spot on BBC TV's *The Old Grey Whistle Test*, playing live in the studio versions of 'Sweet Jesus' and 'Hymn For The Children'. The unusual album title *Time Honoured Ghosts* was suggested by the wife of Harvey Lisberg. Harvey was the band's manager at the time, and the band liked the idea. It's believed that she, in turn, was quoting from elsewhere, possibly a reference to Shakespeare's 'time-honoured Lancaster' in Richard II. Whatever the provenance of its title, *Time Honoured Ghosts* has stood the test of time well, in spite of, or possibly because of, sounding so different to *Everyone Is Everybody Else*. Whilst there may be no obvious standouts to feature in fans' charts of favourite Barclay James Harvest songs, there's very little filler, either, and a number of the tracks have reappeared in recent live sets to great acclaim.

Sleeve Design

The beautiful painting which adorns *Time Honoured Ghosts* has become one of their best-loved album sleeves. Polydor's Paul Welch commissioned freelance artist Bill Dare to come up with a cover design, and it was his idea to create a pastiche of the Maxfield Parrish painting, *Harvest*. He made a rough concept image and submitted that for approval by the band and label, and fortunately everyone liked it. The finished painting covers both back and front of the album cover and can be better appreciated on the gatefold versions of the sleeve which were issued in France and The Netherlands, and on wide-format posters which were issued for promotional purposes and sold at concerts. Original U.K. copies of the LP came with a yellow inner sleeve including all the song lyrics and a photo of the band by Alex Agor. The LP labels are notable for heralding the debut appearance of an iconic logo, designed by Geoff Halpin, who can also take credit for famous logos for the likes of UFO and Genesis. Halpin came up with the classic 'winged woman' emblem, which would be associated with Barclay James Harvest for decades to come, and appear on the labels of several of the band's subsequent albums.

'In My Life' (John Lees)

The album gets off and running with 'In My Life' (no relation to the Beatles song) launching straight in with a cracking lead guitar intro, followed by John's reflections on life in general and the music business in particular. It then changes tack with a weird and wonderful slow middle eight, full of ethereal Mellotron choirs, before John's guitar winds the tempo back up to speed for the finale. We're not let in on the identity of 'Mister middle of the road' who 'reaps what you sow', and John isn't telling, but it's a safe bet that it was someone close to the band at the time ...

'Sweet Jesus' (Les Holroyd)

On the face of it, this almost *a capella* song would seem to have a Christian message, but Les was never a religious man, and the title should probably be seen as more of an exclamation, an expression of the singer's disillusioned and enervated state. The very sparse arrangement is one of its strengths, and John's wonderful 'one-note' solo is the icing on the cake – a perfect example of the old axiom that 'less is more'. A live-in-the-studio version broadcast on BBC TV's *Old Grey Whistle Test* can be heard on the *After The Day -The Radio Broadcasts 1974-1976* double CD and the original album version was also released as a single in The Netherlands in the wake of the success of 'Titles'.

'Titles' (traditional, arranged by John Lees)
A collage of Beatles song titles pieced together by John and embellished with musical quotes chosen by John and Woolly. The titles weren't randomly chosen, as John later explained to the fan club magazine: 'If you listen to the way the titles are laid out, they were picked to try and illustrate the falling out between John Lennon and Paul McCartney.' Perhaps predictably, 'Titles' was chosen by the record company as the most commercial proposition for a single to promote the album. Seen in some quarters as a gimmick or attempted cash-in, the single nevertheless received considerable airplay and made the Top 10 in the Dutch singles chart. 'Titles' also has the distinction of being the only Barclay James Harvest song ever to be released as a single in Japan, where the picture sleeve carried the legend, 'Beatles Forever!' – in Japanese, naturally. The song was revisited on the *Nexus – Barclay James Harvest Through The Eyes Of John Lees* album in 1999, where Woolly added a new verse, casting himself as 'the fool on the hill'.

'Jonathan' (Les Holroyd)
This song has its origins as far back as 1972, in a planned film entitled *Windsong,* about a roadie for a fictional rock group, for which Barclay James Harvest were to compose the soundtrack. The film never reached the production stage, but Les took the part including the line 'like the windsong on the breeze he seems to sigh' for the emotive middle section of 'Jonathan'. The song was inspired by the novel *Jonathan Livingstone Seagull* by Richard Bach, first published in 1972. The book, hugely popular at the time, was a kind of modern-day fable about self-imposed limitations and used the allegory of a seagull breaking free from physical constraints to make its point. In concert settings, a longer version with an extended guitar solo and sound effects panning from one set of speakers to the other and back again really made the song fly (if you'll pardon the expression), and turned it into an immediate live favourite.

'Beyond The Grave' (Woolly Wolstenholme)
Woolly's sole composition to make the cut is a powerful, ambitious piece in the classic Wolstenholme tradition, and was only just written in time for the recording sessions: 'I completed the lyrics to that song on the plane over to America', he explained many years later. 'Elliot Mazer didn't really understand the piece as it wasn't traditional 'rock, man', but upon reflection, I thought it was quite successful'. The title of the song came from an old horror comic, and the original recording went on much longer, but, rather than have a fade-out at the end of the album side, the oddly abrupt ending was achieved by the simple expedient of pressing the stop button on the tape machine! Sadly,

the longer recording doesn't seem to have survived, as it is believed that the original multi-track master tapes for the whole album were lost in the 2008 fire at Universal Studios, Hollywood, which destroyed priceless and irreplaceable recordings by many well-known artists.

'Song For You' (Les Holroyd)

The second side of the vinyl LP opened with another highlight, the stirring 'Song For You'. The dramatic opening guitar riff and bass run are joined by Woolly's keyboards and Mel's powerful, but controlled, drumming to create a superb one-minute introduction before Les's emotive vocals join the mix. The energetic start then gives way to a much quieter, reflective piano-led second half. In an attempt to capture the power and subtlety that Barclay James Harvest possessed on stage, it was decided to record as much as possible of the track live in the studio. That's when the problems started ... As Woolly recalled:

> This led to some difficulties on 'Song For You'. During the quieter second half of the song I had to turn from the organ to the piano and John had to put down his electric guitar and tiptoe across the studio to pick up his acoustic guitar without making a noise. John tried this a number of times without success as his movements were all picked up on tape. When he finally managed it, I hit a bum note! I was not very popular for a few hours after that!

'Hymn For The Children' (John Lees)

John described 'Hymn For The Children' in a contemporary interview with *Sounds* music paper as

> 'like a follow up to 'Child Of The Universe' which is a follow-on from 'Summer Soldier' which is a follow-on from 'Dark Now My Sky' – there's always one statement-type song on each album'.

This particular statement is an attack on racism and discrimination; a plea for equal treatment for all mankind, regardless of colour or creed, and features some particularly fine percussion from Mel and the gorgeous sound of John picking the chords on his iconic sunburst Fender Stratocaster. 'Hymn For The Children' (along with 'Sweet Jesus') was performed live on the *Old Grey Whistle Test*, and the audio recordings of both appear on the *After The Day - The Radio Broadcasts 1974-1976* set. In 2011 the song made a welcome return to live performance at the extremely emotional first concert by John Lees' Barclay James Harvest following the suicide of Woolly Wolstenholme.

'Moongirl' (Les Holroyd)

A beautifully evocative song from Les Holroyd, whose contributions to this album were of the very highest standard. It still has a timeless, romantic feel to it, despite Woolly's typically irreverent on-stage introduction of it at one concert as being 'about groupies – you know, the sort of women who wander around in see-through negligees'! Les was not amused, given that it was actually a heartfelt love song, and the joke was rather lost on the audience, too, as they were in Germany at the time! A novel way of promoting the album was hit upon: the band were filmed 'performing' five of the songs at Pinewood Studios, and then some conceptual footage added later. These included some tasteful shots of a nude girl swimming around to illustrate 'Moongirl', and a rather bizarre gothic sequence for 'Beyond The Grave'. A clip of 'Moongirl' was shown on Granada's *North-West News*, but the other clips were largely unseen until they were unearthed and added to the *Berlin* DVD as 'Time Honoured Tales' thirty-five years later!

'One Night' (John Lees)

The album's closing song tackles the unusual subject of prostitution from the point of view of a customer. John takes a non-judgemental approach, leaving listeners to adopt their own moral stance, and describes the protagonist's feelings with sensitivity and psychological insight. The world-weary flavour of the words finds its counterpart in the music, where the sparse arrangement is set off by some unexpected chords and carefully-woven vocal harmonies. The song was played live on the *Time Honoured Ghosts* and *Octoberon* tours and made a welcome return to live performance thirty-five years later, in 2011, with John Lees' Barclay James Harvest. It was also included as part of an acoustic medley with which the band opened the second half of their shows in 2018.

Octoberon (1976)

Personnel:
John Lees: acoustic guitars, electric guitars, vocals and harmonies
Les Holroyd: acoustic guitars, bass, vocals and harmonies
Woolly Wolstenholme: keyboards and vocals
Mel Pritchard: drums and percussion
Orchestral strings arranged and conducted by Ritchie Close; leader Pat Halling
The Capriol Singers, choir arranged and conducted by Ritchie Close, director Gerald E. Brown
Recorded at Strawberry Studios, Stockport, June to August 1976. Orchestral strings recorded at Chappell Studios, London
Producer: Barclay James Harvest
Engineers: David Rohl and Steve C. Smith (Strawberry); Chris Stone and Terry Davies (Chappell)
Record Label: Polydor (UK and Europe), MCA (USA and Canada)
UK release date: 1 October 1976
Highest chart places: UK: 19, Germany: 40, USA: 174

The original plan had been to combine a coast to coast tour of the United States with the recording of a second studio album at Elliot Mazer's His Master's Wheels in San Francisco. Whilst the tour went ahead as scheduled, taking in more than twenty shows from early March to early April, when the band arrived in San Francisco, Mazer was still busy completing other projects. The band's U.S. working visas were only valid for a limited period, and after several wasted weeks they were forced to return home to England; a new strategy was required. The decision was made to produce the album themselves at Strawberry Studios North in Stockport instead, with the assistance of David Rohl, the Chief Engineer at Strawberry with whom the band had worked previously at Indigo Sound in Manchester. For ten weeks in the long, hot summer of 1976, the band members commuted backwards and forwards to the studio in a battered old Austin Maxi every afternoon, working up until midnight. It quickly became apparent that there was a natural chemistry between Rohl and Barclay James Harvest. Rohl, having previously formed his own progressive group called Mandalaband (most of whose members would go on to form Sad Café), had an empathy with their music, and he was particularly in tune with Woolly Wolstenholme's musical ambitions, which came as a great relief to the keyboard maestro after his disappointing experiences in America. 'David made us sound more like a band on our records', said Woolly. It was Les who came up with the title for the LP: *Octoberon*, a pun on Shakespeare's Oberon, King of the Fairies, since it would be their eighth album, excluding compilations, and was planned for release in October. At the beginning of that month Barclay James Harvest set out on a UK-wide tour to promote the new album, and the hard work soon paid off: the album charted at number 30 on 23 October, and the following week rose to the giddy heights of number 19 – their first Top 20 hit! *Octoberon* also became the band's first record to make an appearance on the German charts, peaking slightly belatedly on New Year's Day, 1977, at number 40.

Sleeve Design

Created by Ian, Charlie and Murray at Brunnings Agency, the sleeve was another superb piece of artwork – embossed on the front was a representation of Oberon, rendered as an androgynous figure holding an orb and sceptre. The image was adapted from an original panel created in 1901 in gilt gesso, painted and set with mother of pearl, by the Edwardian artist Frederick Marriott and was half of a pair. It is believed that the companion piece of Titania is owned by Sir Paul McCartney. The new background to the image continues onto the rear of the cover, surrounding a photo of the band outside a typical Saddleworth farmhouse, with Les shirtless and sporting a large pendant of Oberon's head from the cover image. The same pendant can be seen on a different chest on the inner sleeve which came with original copies of the LP, and the other side of that inner is given over to song lyrics and credits. Unfortunately, the song titles listed on the original album cover are in an apparently random order, although the error was corrected on late reissues. Rather than the traditional Side 1 and Side 2, the 'winged woman' vinyl LP labels bear the legends 'Red Side' and 'Blue Side', in an attempt to group the songs by their general themes. This led to some confusion in some other countries, including Germany, where the sides were reversed: in fact, the first track on the album was always intended to be 'The World Goes On', and 'Suicide?' would be the obvious closer, i.e. the Red Side should be Side 1.

'The World Goes On' (Les Holroyd)

The album opener is notable for featuring the first use of an orchestra on a Barclay James Harvest recording since 'Moonwater' on *Baby James Harvest* some four years earlier. The strings were arranged and conducted by Ritchie Close, who worked with artists such as Maddy Prior, Mandalaband, Big Country, Camel, Jon Astley, The Heebeegeebies (!) and many more until his tragic death in 1991, at the age of 39. The song is one of Les Holroyd's finest compositions, and the soaring strings elevate an already beautiful ballad to the status of a neglected BJH classic, with its simple but highly effective acoustic opening complemented by John's eloquent lead guitar work. Lyrically, the song tackles the subject of life and luck, finishing on an optimistic note with a favourite *leitmotiv* of Les's – flying as an escape (*cf.* 'Jonathan', 'On The Wings Of Love', 'The Life You Lead' and 'Fly Away').

'May Day' (John Lees)

John's first contribution is, like a number of his compositions, lyrically ambiguous, but is primarily an attack on extremism from all sides of the political spectrum. The title refers, of course, to the traditional parades on May 1st, and there are allusions to 'the State' and 'a party man', but elsewhere the words attack simplistic black and white notions of right and wrong. The song can also be read as a description of personal confusion and uncertainty. As John told *Beat Instrumental* magazine the following year:

> I wondered what the reaction of the British people would be to a takeover by a totalitarian regime, and I had a funny idea that everyone reverted to the wartime songs. Instead of doing the arrangements myself, I let someone else do it, and they did this really big choir thing and it got totally out of hand. If I had the experience of self-production then which we have now I would have nipped it in the bud.

The 'big choir thing' to which John referred is the coda to the song, consisting as it does of a choir singing excerpts from six songs (all at the same time) ranging from traditional English pieces such as Elgar's paean to patriotism, 'Land Of Hope And Glory' to the socialist anthem 'The Red Flag'. The other songs included are 'It's A Long Way To Tipperary', 'We'll Meet Again', 'There'll Always Be An England' and 'The White Cliffs Of Dover'. The choir, credited on the inner sleeve as The Capriol Singers, was an ad hoc assemblage, including David Rohl and sound engineer Martin Lawrence.

'Ra' (Woolly Wolstenholme)

Woolly's only compositional contribution to the album is one of his finest, the majestic and grandiose 'Ra'. Inspired by 1976's sweltering (by English standards, at least!) summer, Woolly employed evocative imagery of the Egyptian sun god to capture an atmosphere of intense, shimmering heat. The delicate verses are adorned with some beautifully languid guitar work from John, before a reprise of the opening section leads us to a powerfully dramatic ending. Doubtless David Rohl, with his lifelong interest in Egyptology, approved of the theme, and helped to achieve the semi-classical feel of the recording. Woolly cheerfully admitted to having borrowed the first four notes from one of his favourite classical pieces, Mahler's first symphony, although, as he pointed out, it's hardly a major musical theme in the song.

'Rock 'N' Roll Star' (Les Holroyd)

The Blue side of the original LP opens with Les's song about the trials of making it in the music business, 'Rock 'N' Roll Star'. There's an obvious reference here to The Byrds' 'So You Wanna Be A Rock 'N' Roll Star', and Les's song carries a similar view of the pitfalls of seeking stardom, although musically it is completely different. A more obvious comparison is to The Eagles, and John was clearly aware of that, since his guitar solo bears more than a passing resemblance to 'One Of These Nights'! 'Rock 'N' Roll Star' rapidly became a staple of Barclay James Harvest live sets. It would have made an obvious single, and indeed it was selected as the single for America, where the band were now signed to MCA Records, but curiously, no single was released from the album in Europe. The song did get a chance to shine, though, when it was chosen as the lead track on the following year's *Live EP*, a trailer for the *Live Tapes* album. The EP became the band's first entry on the official U.K. singles chart, making it to number 49, and leading to an appearance on the iconic *Top Of The Pops* TV show. In keeping with BBC policy at the time, the band were prevented from performing the song live in the studio and were forced to mime to a re-recorded studio version taped at Marquee Studios in London two days previously. This shorter 'Top of the Pops' version of 'Rock and Roll Star' is included on remastered CD issues of *Octoberon*.

'Polk Street Rag' (John Lees)

A complete departure for John, 'Polk Street Rag' certainly belongs on the 'blue' side of the album, as it is inspired by the controversial 1972 film *Deep Throat*, starring Linda Lovelace. The film had pretensions to artistic content, and was a massive commercial success at the time, but was basically a pornographic movie about a woman with the unusual anatomical feature of having sexual organs in her throat! Polk Street is in the centre of San Francisco's red-light district and, with the band being underemployed in San Francisco in early 1976, John presumably decided to pass the time by finding out what the fuss was about! The song is actually an uplifting rocker, clearly written with tongue firmly in cheek rather than down throat, and, um, went down well in live concerts, in spite of John's overuse of the fuzz pedal on the predominant guitar riff. The *Live Tapes* recording was used as the B-side of the band's 1978 single, 'Loving Is Easy'.

'Believe In Me' (Les Holroyd)

Les Holroyd's unaccompanied double-tracked vocals introduce 'Believe In Me', a delicate, wistful love song which boasts some beautiful vocal harmonies, comparable with the style of Steve Stills and Manassas on songs like 'It Doesn't Matter', an early influence on Les's writing. John's powerful lead guitar riffs and solo embellish the central 'call and response' section, with the vocals and harmonies alternating between the stereo channels – one to listen to with headphones on! Woolly's Mellotron strings are prominent on the fade-out, recalling the latter part of 'Jonathan' from the previous album, *Time Honoured Ghosts*.

'Suicide?' (John Lees)

Eclipsing 'Polk Street Rag' in the controversiality stakes is the album closer. 'Suicide?' (the question mark, often missed, is vital), sung in the first person, tells the story of someone's final moments before they plunge to their death. It features graphic sound effects achieved by Woolly, wearing a pair of traditional Lancastrian clogs, going up in the service lift at Strawberry Studios, then a dummy, complete with binaural microphones in a specially-designed pair of headphones, being thrown off the top of the Holiday Inn in Manchester for the grisly climax. It's a magnificent, thought-provoking song, with John's macabre humour very much in evidence in the line, 'Don't jump, please for God's sake, let me move my car!' For the sound effects of the atmosphere in the bar at the fictional club 'The Loser', the band's road crew turned thespian. Roadie Murray Thomas, playing the club's bouncer, had to be persuaded to stick to the script and say 'Are you a member?', as we hear on the album, rather than his initial mischievous rendition of it as 'Can I see your member?'! Ian Southerington, the band's live sound engineer, also stars, as a barman, and can be heard asking, 'Can I offer you a drink, Sir?' The song, complete with its beautiful, anthemic keyboard arrangements and memorable guitar solos, quickly established itself as a BJH classic, particularly in concert, where John was most gratified by its reception: 'On that last verse you could hear a pin drop – I was always really impressed with that, people were really listening to it.'

Gone To Earth (1977)

Personnel:
John Lees: acoustic guitar, electric guitar and vocals
Les Holroyd: acoustic guitar, bass, banjo and vocals
Woolly Wolstenholme: keyboards and vocals
Mel Pritchard: drums and percussion
Recorded at Strawberry Studios, Stockport, March to June 1977.
Producer: Barclay James Harvest, Co-Produced by David Rohl
Engineers: David Rohl, assisted by Richard Scott
Mastering Engineer: Ian Cooper at Utopia Blue Room
Record Label: Polydor (UK and Europe), MCA (USA and Canada)
UK release date: September 1977
Highest chart places: UK: 30, Germany: 10

Having enjoyed a productive working and creative working relationship with David Rohl during the recording of *Octoberon*, it was a logical move to draft David in as co-producer for the follow-up album. Work began in March 1977, and members of a newly formed fan club run by Woolly's wife, Jill, and called Friends Of Barclay James Harvest, were given an insight into the recording process:

> The next album is currently being made at Strawberry Studios in Stockport on a 24 track machine. So far, we are still working on the backing tracks which usually consist of guitar, bass and drums and occasionally, a keyboard. On some of these tracks we have done the preliminary instrument overdubs (i.e.: additional instruments laid on top of the basic tracks), but these are not necessarily the final additions, but are used as arrangement guides. As yet, there are only rough vocals.

Determined to avoid one or two mistakes which they felt had been made with *Octoberon*, the band opted for more and shorter songs, with less grandiose arrangements. The end result was an album which is highly rated by fans to this day. Released in late September 1977, it entered the U.K. charts at number 30 on 1 October, but rather disappointingly failed to climb any higher, although it did remain in the Top 50 for six weeks. In Germany, it was a different story: on the back of a sell-out German tour, demand having been stoked by the cancellation of the previous year's German dates when John fell ill, the album entered the chart on 15 December at number 29, but then refused to go away, staying on the German album chart for an incredible 181 continuous weeks, including three separate Top 10 appearances during 1979 and 1980. Almost overnight, it seemed, Barclay James Harvest had become superstars in Germany, and the album also fared well in neighbouring Switzerland. The band, too, were happy with the results of their labours, with Woolly looking back fondly:

> A lot of good things came together on Gone To Earth – some of John's best,

> like 'Poor Man's Moody Blues' and 'Hymn' and Les's 'Spirit On The Water'. There was a nice balance, the artwork was good and somehow everything happened at the right time.

One for trivia fans: Cathy, who is thanked along with Peter (Tattersall) on the back cover of the LP, is Cathy Redfern, the receptionist at Strawberry Studios who can be heard whispering 'Be quiet, big boys don't cry' on 10cc's massive 1975 hit, 'I'm Not In Love'.

Sleeve Design

The beautiful and innovative cutaway sleeve was designed by Maldwyn Reece Tootill, a freelance illustrator who had become friendly with the band. Mel Pritchard had already purchased and commissioned several of his works, but Mal had never designed an LP cover before. He explained how it came about:

> After securing a vote of confidence from the band, I set about developing some ideas. I used to meet the band in the Hanging Gate pub on a regular basis when I came up from London and this was where much of the business was done! Several titles were kicked about and I proposed Gone To Earth, which was evocative of the owl striking its prey as it descends to earth. I can't fully recall how the cutaway cover emerged, but I do recall feeling quite pleased with myself at innovating the concept of using the inner sleeve or bag as a fundamental part of the illustration, and one which carried an alternative image on the reverse side, showing a dawn scene in contrast to the dusk image which formed the main concept image. Being a young and inexperienced illustrator at the time I was blissfully unaware of the production problems inherent in producing the cover in this way, and to this day I'm eternally grateful for the band's support throughout the project in the face of some initial shock-horror responses from Joe Mirowski, the art director at Polydor.

The montage on the back of the LP sleeve was created by David Rohl and the band, using photographs taken by Les Holroyd's brother-in-law, Christopher B. Roberts.

'Hymn' (John Lees)

The song which has come to be regarded by many as *the* definitive BJH classic, rivalled only by 'Mocking Bird', had an inauspicious beginning, having been rejected for inclusion on *Barclay James Harvest And Other Short Stories* way back in 1971. Starting gently with acoustic guitars, the song builds steadily to an inspirational peak, augmented by massed twelve-string guitars, organ and horns. The religious symbolism of the lyrics led many listeners to assume that the song was a Christian anthem or even a Christmas song, but, as with many of John's songs, the surface meaning is only half the story. The working title of the song during the recording sessions was 'Hymn For A White Lady', and referred to the slang name for cocaine. The lyrics draw unfavourable comparisons between chemically induced 'highs' and those of a spiritual nature, as John explained in a contemporary interview with the *Daily Mirror*:

> I'm not a religious freak and I don't go to church, but I do believe in God and I also believe that He is preferable to cocaine. Part of my lyrics say 'don't try to fly, you know you might not come down', in other words, you might take an overdose and die.

The title was shortened because of understandable concerns that the longer title might be misinterpreted as being pro rather than anti-drugs. 'Hymn' was issued as a single in a picture sleeve on 22 July 1977, in advance of the album. Unfortunately, the BBC considered it 'too Christmassy', and so the sales push was postponed until later in the year. In Germany, the response was much more positive, and the song received a great deal of airplay, helping its parent album into the charts. 'Hymn' took over from 'Mocking Bird' as the grand finale of the band's live act, which it remains, with very few exceptions, to this day. It still gets played regularly on the radio in Germany, and, ironically, at Christmas time in the U.K. In 2018 'Hymn' reached a brand new audience when it was covered by Sarah Brightman, and became a single and the title track of her new studio album, which went to number 1 on the U.S. *Billboard* Classical Albums chart.

'Love Is Like A Violin' (John Lees)

In the Friends Of Barclay James Harvest fan club newsletter announcing the song titles for the forthcoming *Gone To Earth* album, Woolly's wife, Jill, was at pains to point out that 'Love Is Like A Violin' is 'Nothing like the Ken Dodd song, I'm very glad to report'! John's composition is a bittersweet romantic ballad, using the metaphor of the changing seasons to chart the blossoming and withering of a love affair. Curiously, the verse 'Love was like a summer breeze, after pouring rain, blowing all the clouds away, bringing sun again', which was printed on the inner sleeve of the LP, does not appear on the actual recording. The song had, presumably, been truncated in line with the policy of keeping things short and concise. In later years nobody could remember whether the missing verse had actually been recorded at the time, but it has never surfaced in the record company tape libraries, so we must assume not.

'Friend Of Mine' (Les Holroyd)

Les's up-tempo, country-influenced number was chosen as the follow-up single to 'Hymn', and has, perhaps because of the overall very high standard of the songs on this album, been rather neglected. The lyrics are generally interpreted as being about the end of a relationship, but there is also an element of another of Les's favourite themes, life on the road as a rock musician. For the single, the recording was remixed to give it a brighter, more radio-friendly sound, and both mixes can be found on remastered CDs of the album. The song showcases a rare glimpse of Les's talents on the banjo, an instrument which received another airing when 'Friend Of Mine' was re-introduced into live sets by Barclay James Harvest Featuring Les Holroyd in 2012.

'Poor Man's Moody Blues' (John Lees)

Lazy journalistic put-downs of Barclay James Harvest as 'the poor man's Moody Blues', largely based on the fact that both groups featured a lot of Mellotron, were nothing new. However, a concert review in the *New Musical Express* which was published mid-way through the *Octoberon* tour was the last straw for John, as it not only trotted out the same old comparisons but also went on to insult the band's audience. In the liner notes for 2003's remastered CD of *Gone To Earth*, John described his reaction:

> I went back to my hotel room that night and started messing around with a chord structure that reminded me of 'Nights in White Satin'. I was so pissed off with this journalist that I sat down and wrote most of 'Poor Man's Moody Blues' that night.

John told *Beat Instrumental* magazine how he approached it:

> I took the skeleton structure of 'Nights In White Satin' – just that drum beat, and put a new melody to it – you listen to it and you think you're listening to 'Nights In White Satin', with the same breaks and everything, but the moment you try singing that melody you'll find it doesn't work at all.

Ironically, 'Poor Man's Moody Blues' took on a life of its own, becoming one of the most popular songs in the band's repertoire, not least in Germany, and in Greece it has even become a popular song to accompany newlyweds down the aisle! Not everyone, though, was a fan. Les Holroyd told *Prog* magazine in August 2016:

> I met Justin Hayward a long time after we'd done that song and we had a chat about it. He wasn't too pleased about that song. I can understand why. For me, it was never funny or clever in the first place. John Lees wrote it, and I was uncomfortable recording the song. I wish we'd never done it.

Les may have disliked the song, but its popularity was undeniable, and three months after giving that interview, Les reintroduced 'Poor Man's Moody Blues' into his own band's live sets.

'Hard Hearted Woman' (Les Holroyd)

The second side of the original long player opened with Les Holroyd's tale of being bewitched by love for an unfeeling siren, set to a mid-tempo beat with John's twin-tracked guitar riff and Woolly's keyboards to the fore. The instrumental break towards the end is surprisingly funky for a Barclay James Harvest song, and that was particularly true of the extended version to which audiences were treated on the 1977 tour. On the album, the song slowly fades and segues into ...

'Sea Of Tranquility' (Woolly Wolstenholme)

This is Woolly Wolstenholme's only composition to appear on *Gone To Earth*, but is possibly his finest contribution ever to a Barclay James Harvest album. Starting quietly, the piece develops rapidly towards a big finish and is a classic, keyboard-led prog-rock epic (if a four-minute song can be described as an epic!). With the benefit of hindsight, it's not difficult to see that the lyrics, ostensibly about the futility of the space race in the 1960s and 1970s, also reflect the writer's growing dissatisfaction within the band. 'Our hopes ever high that the songs we sing and the words we bring should never die' speaks of a 'star-struck' optimism, but 'We sold our souls for senseless gain and brought our harvest home in vain' lay bare the bitterness of disillusionment. Whilst this was not Woolly's final album with Barclay James Harvest, there can be little doubt that he was already well on the way towards his decision to leave.

'Spirit On The Water' (Les Holroyd)

Returning to a regular Barclays preoccupation with environmental issues, which can be traced right through from 'Dark Now My Sky' to 'Stand Up', the delicate 'Spirit On The Water' takes a sideswipe at the slaughter of seal pups on behalf of the fur industry and those who wear its products. The lovely melody and gorgeous harmonies sweeten the pill of the hard-hitting lyrics of one of Les's best and most affecting songs:

> A sacrifice for the coat he's wearing
> A 'paradise' for the lady
> Who dares colour him red upon the snow?

'Leper's Song' (John Lees)

John Lees has long been an avid reader, so it's not surprising that several of his songs have been inspired by books, or, in the case of 'Leper's Song', two books: Graham Greene's *A Burnt-Out Case*, which is set in a leper colony and deals with so-called burn-out syndrome, and *An Outcast Of The Islands* by Joseph Conrad, which has a similar theme of one man's alienation from the society in which he finds himself. The song is the most energetic on what is generally a rather lush album, but, perhaps surprisingly, has never been performed live.

'Taking Me Higher' (Les Holroyd)

The final track on Side Two of the LP was the gentle Les Holroyd composition, 'Taking Me Higher', employing a wash of lovely vocal harmonies to close the album on a simple but, um, uplifting note. In concert, the song was extended with a great John Lees guitar solo and a typical Woolly Wolstenholme minor finish, making for a more satisfactory ending than the slightly anticlimactic fade out on the album.

Related Songs:

'Our Kid's Kid' (John Lees)

Released as the B-side of 'Hymn', 'Our Kid's Kid' was recorded at the same time as the *Gone To Earth* tracks, but didn't make the cut for the album. It's an autobiographical piece about John's family, a sprightly song with a country feel, written to mark the occasion of his older sister Edna giving birth to her daughter, Ruth. 'Our kid' is a common expression in Northern England for a brother or sister, especially a younger one, while the 'race' between John and Edna was to be the first to give their parents grandchildren. Among the names and places mentioned in the lyrics, Bargap Road was their parents' home in Oldham Edge, Frederick was the name of John's father, Frank was a relative of Edna's husband and Peter (Tattersall) was the manager of Strawberry Studios and a family friend.

'Lied' (John Lees)

One more song was recorded at the *Gone To Earth* sessions, but was also left off the album in the final accounting, probably because of the time limitations peculiar to vinyl LPs: 'Lied', also known as 'Please Give Me One More Chance', is a John Lees song with a twist, about a relationship in difficulties, and bears all the hallmarks of the BJH sound of the time. Abandoned during the recording sessions when only partly completed, with John singing a rough take and no backing vocals or other overdubs, it was rediscovered in the vaults in the next century and took its place on the remastered versions of the *Gone To Earth* CD. The line in the lyrics about 'when my blessings number five' may be a reference to the ancient Chinese tradition of *Wu Fu*, or the five bats of happiness, which symbolise the five blessings: first, longevity; second, wealth; third, health and peace; fourth, doing good; and fifth, enjoying a ripe old age and a peaceful end.

XII (1978)

Personnel:
John Lees: electric and acoustic guitars, bass and vocals
Les Holroyd: electric and acoustic guitars, bass, piano, double bass, banjo and vocals
Woolly Wolstenholme: piano, Mellotron, synthesizers, Hammond organ, 12-string guitars and vocals
Mel Pritchard: drums, percussion, glockenspiel, tubular bells, vibraphone
Mike Timoney (misspelt as Timony in the album credits): Cordovox accordion on 'The Closed Shop'
Recorded at Strawberry Studios, Stockport, March to July 1978.
Producer: Barclay James Harvest and Martin Lawrence
Engineers: Martin Lawrence (recording and mixing), Chris Nagle (tape assistant)
Mastering Engineer: Melvyn Abrahams at Strawberry Mastering, London
Record Label: Polydor
UK release date: 29 September 1978
Highest chart places: UK: 31, Germany: 18, Switzerland: 4

On 13 March 1978, the band members gathered at Strawberry Studios to review and select material for their next studio effort. The recording of *Gone To Earth* with David Rohl at Strawberry having been so successful, it was natural that for their next album the band wanted to repeat the formula. All went well, to begin with, the band choosing to go for a more 'live' sound in the studio, in an attempt to get a less clinical, more energetic result, and reporting in their fan club newsletter that this method was promoting more interaction between the band members and producing a constant flow of ideas. Unfortunately, the recording sessions coincided with the build-up to the release of David's own project, a concept album called *The Eye Of Wendor: Prophecies*, issued under the name of his old group, Mandalaband. Ironically, the members of Barclay James Harvest were themselves amongst the many guest musicians featured on it, but now it became a source of discord as Rohl's conflicting priorities disrupted the recording of the new BJH album.

The consequent arguments resulted in Rohl's departure, leaving the recording sessions in limbo. Strawberry's manager, Peter Tattersall, stepped in for a few days until a replacement was found in Martin Lawrence, best-known for his work on Godley and Creme's *Consequences* set. In the event, the departure of David Rohl as co-producer didn't have a significant effect on the final sound, since much of the work had been completed before he and the band parted company. The working title of the album was *High*, and at one point it was planned to use a photo of a sunset taken by Woolly from an aircraft as the cover design. In the end, the title was rejected as it could be taken as a drug reference, and the plan was jettisoned, although the photo would go on to adorn the sleeve of Woolly's solo album, *Mæstoso*, two years later. Instead, they went with the title *XII*, partly because it would mark the band's twelfth anniversary together, and partly because it would be their twelfth album (if two live LPs and the compilation *Early Morning Onwards* are included in the tally). Released on 15 September 1978, its reception demonstrated the widening gap between the band's popularity in Germany and in the U.K. – at home, where punk and New Wave were at their peak, *XII* made only a fleeting appearance in the UK album chart at number 31. In Germany, however, despite peaking at a relatively low number 18, *XII* stayed on the album chart for months, selling a quarter of a million copies in its first year to become the band's second German gold disc. In spite of its success, *XII* had a difficult act to follow, with its predecessor still riding high in the German charts. Woolly summed up his feelings thus:

> Things seem to have happened in twos; I felt that Other Short Stories was overshadowed by Once Again, and XII was overshadowed by the success of Gone To Earth, although sonically they are more of a pair. I personally think that some of the songs on XII are better.

Sleeve Design

Mal Tootill, who had designed the outstanding cover for *Gone To Earth*, was approached to come up with another design for the new studio album and produced a mock-up entitled *Thunder In The Skies*. This depicted a field of wheat with a tortoiseshell butterfly on an ear of corn in the foreground. The faces of John, Les, Mel and Woolly were then included in the butterfly wings, an idea which had come from the band members themselves. However, the Barclays were looking for something less pastoral and chose not to use this design. Another local artist, Chris Clover, was recommended to Woolly, and came up with the 'earth from space' image, then incorporated the butterfly with the faces in the wings. In order to avoid conflict and possible delays to the album over the similarities with Mal Tootill's design, it was agreed that Mal Tootill would be credited with the concept, and Chris Clover with the actual artwork. UK copies of *XII* also included a large fold-out poster with the cover design on one side and lyrics and credits on the back, although Polydor omitted to include this in the first batch pressed. Other European pressings sported a less lavish fold-out insert with the album artwork on the outside and lyrics inside.

'Fantasy: Loving Is Easy' (John Lees)

The first song on the album was also chosen as the single to promote it – a logical choice, given its infectious guitar riff, toe-tapping rhythm and memorable chorus, which would quickly make it a crowd favourite in concert. However, as a single it became the cause of some controversy, verging on farce. When 'Loving Is Easy' was previewed to the BBC for inclusion on the Radio One playlist, there was a problem: they loved the song, but felt that lyrics such as 'I shoot all my love into you/in your fire' were a shade too risqué for daytime radio's squeaky-clean image. The band agreed to re-record the vocals, substituting the more innocuous, 'I send all my love out to you' and 'I burn all my love in your fire', and were rewarded with an invitation to record the song for *Top Of The Pops*. Having done so, they looked forward to heavy airplay and TV coverage giving them their first major hit single, only to discover that the BBC had banned the song anyway! The reason? Auntie Beeb cited another line in the song, which goes 'Just get a hold and watch how it grows'!! Had things turned out differently, BJH's staid image could have been banished forever! The (insufficiently!) bowdlerised version was available as a limited edition pressed in blue vinyl and is included on remastered CD versions of the album.

'Berlin' (Les Holroyd)

Les's first contribution to the album is rightly regarded as another Barclays classic by the band's fans. It was inspired by the plight of the eponymous city, which, at the time the song was written, was divided by the infamous Wall separating East and West Berlin. The western half of the city was thus left high and dry as an 'island', entirely surrounded by the Communist German Democratic Republic (DDR), until the wall finally fell in 1989. The plaintive piano was played by Les, both on the record and in subsequent live performances, with John taking over Les's accustomed role on bass.

'Classics: A Tale Of Two Sixties' (John Lees)

The observant will have noticed that all of the John Lees song titles on this album are prefaced by literary genres, the idea being that they would be presented like different shelves of a library. For the 'classics', John takes an affectionate stance in this engaging look back at some of his early inspirations, starting with the punning Dickensian title. The later influences referred to in the lyrics include *Easy Rider*, the film whose soundtrack featured The Byrds, plus Bob Dylan's Rolling Thunder Revue, Frank Zappa, The Who, David Bowie and Arthur Lee of the band Love, whose classic *Forever Changes* album was a huge favourite in the formative days of BJH – they even performed covers of 'Andmoreagain', 'A House Is Not A Motel' and 'Old Man' in their early live shows. 'Chairman Young', whose thoughts were credited with inspiring the song, worked with the band's manager, John Crowther, and first introduced them to the music of bands like Love.

'Turning In Circles' (Les Holroyd)

With a similar lyrical theme to 'Hard Hearted Woman', 'Turning In Circles' returns to the perils of meeting strange women on the road, possibly during one of Les and Mel's forays into local nightlife, as captured by the *Caught Live* documentary film. This depicted life on the road for band and crew on the previous year's German tour. The song is simple and catchy, and sees Les's writing turning in a more commercial direction: in some ways it has the feel of a precursor to 'Life Is For Living'.

'Fact: The Closed Shop' (John Lees)

John courts controversy again with 'The Closed Shop', written about the then-prevalent agreements between trade unions and management whereby nobody would be allowed to hold a particular job unless they were a member of the relevant union. The lyrics were taken by some as reactionary, although John Peel made the observation on air that it was difficult to tell whether John was pro or anti; in a later interview John denied that he had been union-bashing, explaining:

> I wasn't against the working class, I wasn't against the unions – I was against the closed shop. I thought it was a destructive force, and I still do. If you look back through all the songs I've written in that kind of vein, they're all pro-working class, because that's what I am, and you can't change where you come from. I'm not really political; I've got a social conscience.

Musically, the song is memorable for its distinct marching band drumming from Mel Pritchard, with the underscored melody line played by John on overdubbed recorders, and a guest appearance from Manchester musician Mike Timoney (not 'Timony' as in the album credits) playing something called a Cordovox behind the verses. The Cordovox was a kind of electronic accordion which sounds a little like an early synthesizer. Mike's work can also be heard on records by Hotlegs, 10cc, China Crisis and The Icicle Works, as well as his own 1971 album of cover versions entitled *The Astounding Sound Of The Cordovox*.

'In Search Of England' (Woolly Wolstenholme)

Woolly described his haunting 'In Search Of England' as being 'about youth and principles on one hand and the voice of experience on the other, a kind of father and son thing.' Written in the form of a dialogue between 'The Boy' and 'The Old Man', it's one of Woolly's most memorable songs, widely regarded as an absolute highlight of his time with Barclay James Harvest. It would return to live sets with Mæstoso and with John Lees' Barclay James Harvest, where it was fondly referred to as 'Church Of England'! Despite the running order of songs on the LP, this was one of the last songs to be completed on the album and would prove to be the last that Woolly ever recorded with Barclay James Harvest.

'Sip Of Wine' (Les Holroyd)

Another cautionary tale, this time of the perils of being seduced by groupies and loving it! Les's playful and tongue-in-cheek song includes the delightful piece of wordplay, 'I held her breath and she was holding mine!'. We held our own collective breath in shock ... The song was particularly satisfying in its more vigorous live form, and was one of many highlights at the apogee of the group's popularity, the massive free concert in Berlin on 30 August 1980.

'Harbour' (Woolly Wolstenholme)

Written about 'coming home on a plane from some monstrous tour, or from America', Woolly's other contribution to the album encapsulates the relief of returning to the haven of a loved one after an exhausting and depressing experience. Early in the proceedings it was considered as a single and was therefore recorded at a fast tempo, but then slowed down for use solely as an album track when the plan changed. Woolly felt that the song 'lost some attack in the process', and certainly it gained a new lease of life when it finally became a fixture in live performances from 1999 right up until Woolly's untimely death in 2010.

'Science Fiction: Nova Lepidoptera' (John Lees)
The distinctive Morse code at the beginning of 'Nova Lepidoptera', which has also been used at various times as a very effective introduction to live concerts, spells out, appropriately enough, 'U.F.O.'. Stuck for inspiration for lyrics, John turned to his own bookshelves and his collection of science-fiction novels. Taking titles and fragments from some of his favourite books, such as Arthur C. Clarke's *The Deep Range* and *Ringworld* by Larry Niven, he wove them into a very effective lyric, and the twin lead guitars turn the piece into a standout track. The song quickly became another live favourite and remains so to this day.

'Giving It Up' (Les Holroyd)
'Giving it Up' is a very atmospheric ballad, with masses of multi-tracked backing vocals by John and Les lending the piece a spiritual, almost elegiac feel. The slightly melancholic lyrics, in combination with the 'heavenly choirs', add to the haunting impression, making it another highlight on what is already a strong set of songs.

'Fiction: The Streets Of San Francisco' (John Lees)
The album bows out with 'The Streets Of San Francisco', inspired by the American film and TV detective series of the same name, starring Karl Malden and Michael Douglas. The lyrics tell a fictional tale set in the city, namechecking the neighbourhood of Haight(-Ashbury) and the Golden Gate bridge across 'Frisco Bay' along the way. It's an unusual song in the BJH catalogue, lyrically and musically, and rather underrated. It's also notable for being topped and tailed by a rare example of Woolly Wolstenholme's evocative harmonica playing.

Eyes Of The Universe (1979)

Personnel:
John Lees: guitars and vocals
Les Holroyd: guitars, bass, keyboards and vocals
Mel Pritchard: drums and percussion
Kevin McAlea: Grand piano and Mini Moog on 'The Song (They Love To Sing)'; Yamaha CS80 and C3 Hammond organ on 'Sperratus'
Alan Fawkes: Saxophone on 'Play To The World'
Recorded at Strawberry Studios, Stockport, July to September 1979.
Producer: Barclay James Harvest and Martin Lawrence
Engineer: Martin Lawrence (recording and re-mixing)
Assisted by: Richard Scott, Chris Nagle and Glenn Mackintosh
Mastering Engineer: Melvyn Abrahams at Strawberry Mastering, London
Record Label: Polydor
UK release date: 5 November 1979
Highest chart places: Germany: 3, Switzerland: 1, France: 22, Norway: 6

On 23 March 1979, the band signed a new management contract with Handle Artists, formalising their relationship with long-time booking agent Lindsay Brown and bringing in David Walker as business manager. Walker first came to prominence in the music business as manager of The Sweet, whilst Brown had been their agent, and also represented Barclay James Harvest for Harvey Lisberg's Kennedy Street Enterprises. With the business side of their affairs on a more certain footing, it was time to think about the next studio album. The band began 'routining' (trying out) new material, planning to convene at Strawberry Studios in July and begin recording. Eight songs were selected: three from John ('Capricorn', 'Sperratus' and 'Skin Flicks'), three from Les (in instrumental form, the songs which would eventually become 'Play To The World', 'The Song (They Love To Sing)' and 'Rock 'N' Roll Lady') and two of Woolly's ('Lives On The Line' and 'A Prospect Of Whitby') – his 'American Excess' was rejected as 'too pretentious'! Once again, though, the plan did not go smoothly. As Woolly put it in a later interview,

> We went into rehearsals and we started to trot through 'Capricorn' or something, and it just ... the bottom went out of it all, it felt so pointless. It had been something that I'd been running up to for a while, and my heart just wasn't in it any more. I just didn't want to go on.

To the consternation of the rest of the BJH camp, Woolly walked out, and could not be persuaded to change his mind. He would honour his commitment to four big German shows which had already been booked for late June and early July, but he would not be part of the new album. John put a brave face on it, telling German magazine *Pop/Melody Maker* in November 1979:

Above: Saving water! Bath time at Preston House, 1968. (*John Lees*)

Left: All say cheese ... First studio photoshoot, March 1968. *(The Cherry Red Archive)*

Right: An interesting selection of classical instruments on Saddleworth Moor, April 1968. *(The Cherry Red Archive)*

Right: The debut single, 'Early Morning', April 1968. *(EMI Records)*

Left: Windswept on the moors - photoshoot for the debut album, 1970. *(The Cherry Red Archive)*

Left: Nautical EMI publicity shot by the River Thames, 1971. (*The Cherry Red Archive*)

Right: *Once Again* album cover, February 1971. *(EMI Records)*

Left: Rehearsals for *And Other Short Stories*, 1971. (*The Cherry Red Archive*)

Right: Wally Allen (front), Norman Smith (behind Wally to the left, standing), Martyn Ford (to the right of Wally, seated) and the orchestra on the roof of EMI's Manchester Square headquarters in London during the recording of *And Other Short Stories* in 1971. (*The Cherry Red Archive*)

Left: Pastoral photo session for *And Other Short Stories*, 1971. (*The Cherry Red Archive*)

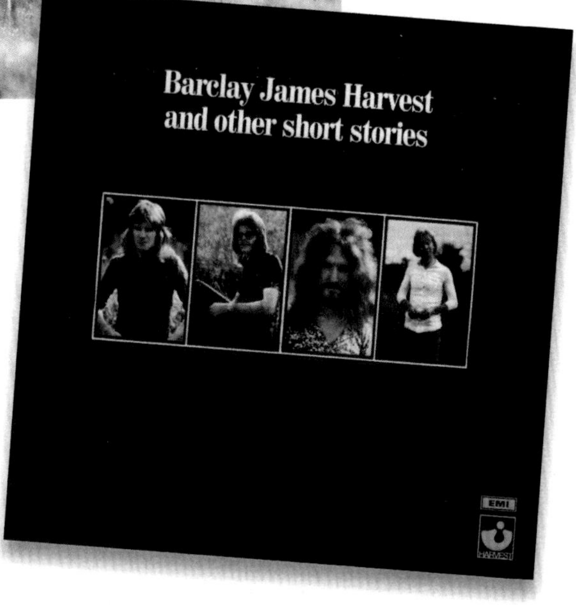

Right: *Barclay James Harvest And Other Short Stories* album cover, November 1971. *(EMI Records)*

Left: 1972 promo photo used for the *Early Morning Onwards* compilation LP. (*The Cherry Red Archive*)

Below: On stage with the orchestra, September 1972. (*The Cherry Red Archive*)

Right: John on stage, circa 1973. (*The Cherry Red Archive*)

Left: Woolly in action, circa 1973. (*The Cherry Red Archive*)

Left: *Barclay James Harvest Live* album cover, November 1974. (*Polydor Records*)

Right: *Time Honoured Ghosts* album cover, October 1975. (*Polydor Records*)

Left: *Octoberon* album cover, October 1976. (*Polydor Records*)

Right: 'Hymn' picture sleeve single, July 1977. (*Polydor Records*)

Left: *Gone To Earth* album cover, September 1977. (*Polydor Records*)

Right: *XII* album cover, September 1978. (*Polydor Records*)

Above: 1976 tour promo with Marcel Avram and Marek Lieberberg of German tour promoters, MAMA Concerts. (*Polydor Records*)

Left: Mel on the Octoberon tour, October 1976. (*Mike Muller*)

Above: Photomontage sent out with the *XII* promotional press packs in 1978. (*Polydor Records*)

Right: *Eyes Of The Universe* album cover, November 1979. (*Polydor Records*)

Above: The legendary concert on the steps of the Berlin Reichstag, 30 August 1980. (*Polydor Records*)

Left: *Turn Of The Tide* album cover, May 1981. (*Polydor Records*)

Right: Presentation of German gold discs for *Live Tapes* and *Turn Of The Tide* at the Sturmhaube building in Kampen, Sylt, 1981. (*Polydor Records*)

Left: *A Concert For The People (Berlin)* album cover, July 1982. (*Polydor Records*)

Left: Colourful 'Just A Day Away' butterfly-shaped UK picture disc, May 1983. (*Polydor Records*)

Right: Victims of circumstance, that's what we are! Promotional photo, taken at the time of the 1984 recording sessions. (*Polydor Records*)

Left: Promotional postcard from 1990 for *Welcome To The Show*. (*Polydor Records*)

Left: Photoshoot at the UCL Observatory, Mill Hill, London, 1990, complete with genuine autographs! (*Polydor Records*)

Right: 'Backstage' before an open-air amphitheatre concert at the Freilichtbühne Heppenheim, June 1993. (*Keith Domone*)

Above: A well-deserved tea break outside Friarmere Studios during the recording of *River Of Dreams*, June 1996. (*Monika Domone*)

Below: John Lees' Barclay James Harvest and orchestra, Athens Odeon of Herodes Atticus, September 2018. (*Jez Smith*)

> At first, the split affected me a lot. Woolly and I had been best friends from very early on. But then, when the big breakthrough was about to happen, Woolly didn't want to be part of it any more. More and more often we had musical differences – Les, Mel and I wanted to widen the musical horizon of the band, but Woolly wanted to stick to the old BJH sound and go even further into the classical direction. I wanted to throw in the towel. Without Woolly I didn't see any future for the band. Now I've got over the split and see the positive side of it. The eternal arguments with Woolly are finally a thing of the past. When we recorded the new LP, which we did without Woolly, we noticed how much easier it was suddenly. At last, it was real fun making music together.

Les was more sanguine about the split. When asked in 1990 how Woolly's departure had affected his role within the Barclays, he replied:

> Not a lot, to be honest. We'd always all of us played guitars and keyboards, so even in the days when Woolly was there a lot of the keyboard stuff was done by myself and John. From that point of view getting our personal ideas across was much easier. In recording I could take my song in and play it rather than having to say to someone how I wanted it and having to compromise.

Mel had mixed feelings:

> I think at the beginning there was this terrible shock, and then I think we were all a little bit petrified about going into the studio. Obviously, it left a massive hole, but I think as often happens you tend to close ranks.

Two additional songs were chosen to replace Woolly's contributions, one each from Les and John. Les stood in on keyboards, with assistance from guest musician Kevin McAlea (ex-Bees Make Honey and a member of Kate Bush's touring band). The album was completed by September and released by Polydor at the beginning of November. Once again, reaction to the record highlighted the ever-growing disparity between the band's status in the UK and the rest of Europe: at home, it was the band's first album in five years to fail to chart at all, whilst in Switzerland, it went to number one, and in Norway, it made the top ten. On its German release, *Eyes Of The Universe* climbed to number three in the album chart, going gold within three months and selling over three hundred thousand copies.

Sleeve Design

The cover was designed by Alwyn Clayden, who was an art director at Polydor, using photographs by John Shaw. The futuristic artwork incorporates what appear to be flying saucers, but is lent an interesting twist by the fact that the UFOs can also be seen as windows looking out onto another world. Original UK copies had a black and white lyric inner sleeve, and a butterfly embossed on the bottom right corner of the front – this is missing from some later issues, including Polydor CDs, misleading some fans into thinking that the band's trademark butterfly didn't appear on the album.

'Love On The Line' (Les Holroyd)

When it was first presented, like all of Les's songs, in demo form without any lyrics, 'Love On The Line' was rejected as a candidate for the album. However, it was hastily reinstated on Woolly's departure, with replacements required for Woolly's compositions. Once completed and recorded, 'Love On The Line' was selected as a single to promote the album, becoming the band's second UK singles chart entry, albeit at a modest number 63. Ironically, the title chosen for it was similar to Woolly's 'Lives On The Line', the song which it replaced. Like Woolly's 'bit of bizarre in 6/8', Les's synth-looped offering, on which he played all of the keyboards himself, is a fairly rocky number, but the theme here is the consuming power of love.

'Alright Down Get Boogie (Mu Ala Rusic)' (John Lees)

John's 'new' one was also a former reject in its earlier guise of 'Ride, Cowboy, Ride!'. The original song, penned with John's tongue firmly lodged in cheek, described a fictional encounter with a transvestite in a night club. The subject matter was, sadly, deemed inappropriate for Barclay James Harvest, so the lyrics were completely re-written to create 'Alright Down Get Boogie (Mu Ala Rusic)'. The subtitle, an anagram of 'aural music', is actually sung in the piece, a rare (praise be!) stab at sexy disco beats. In its re-written form, it's still mildly risqué, if not as amusing as the original incarnation. It's not surprising that it didn't make the first cut for the album, as it has to be said that this is one of John's weaker offerings.

'The Song (They Love To Sing)' (Les Holroyd)

Les was clearly in full ballad mode whilst composing for this album, as he came up with not one, but two of his very best. 'The Song (They Love To Sing)' is the more interesting of the two in its musical structure, with some lines in the verses starting a beat early, using the same syllable and note as the end of the preceding line. It works very well, but the song has been rather neglected down the years in favour of the similar, but more crowd-pleasing, 'Play To The World'. The grand piano and mini Moog on 'The Song (They Love To Sing)' were played by Kevin McAlea.

'Skin Flicks' (John Lees)

It's plain to see that John was going through a phase of writing a few playfully provocative songs towards the end of the seventies (*cf.* 'Loving Is Easy' and 'Ride, Cowboy Ride') – what Woolly described as 'John's smutty ones'. Here we have another example, its title a slang term for pornographic films, and the lyrics a morality tale about a model whose career as a glamour pin-up comes between her and the narrator. Like all such judgemental stories, it doesn't end well, until she's 'suntanned right down to the bone, and our love's gone'. Musically, John continues where 'Poor Man's Moody Blues' leaves off, with the coda cheekily borrowing a brief riff from the Moody Blues' 'Question'.

'Sperratus' (John Lees)

Much more in the classic Barclay James Harvest tradition is the song which led off the flip side of the LP, John's classic duelling guitar-driven 'Sperratus'. He must have been fond of crosswords at the time, as the title is another anagram, this time of 'superstar' – appropriately enough since the song tackles the often complex relationship between stars and the fans who put them in that position. The lyrics also, indirectly, provided the album with its title: 'Look in my eyes / See the light of the universe'.

Several of the album tracks were edited down in the studio for possible use as singles, 'Sperratus' being one of them, but it was never issued as a single. Today it retains only an unfairly obscure place in the BJH pantheon, in spite of some superb live performances of it during the band's concerts between 1980 and 1982. The previously unreleased edited version of this, and of 'Rock 'N' Roll Lady' and 'Play To The World', were included as bonus tracks on later, remastered CDs of the album.

'Rock 'N' Roll Lady' (Les Holroyd)

Les's upbeat paean to the music business and its camp followers, 'Rock 'N' Roll Lady', is next up, with an intro reminiscent of 'Don't Fear The Reaper'. Les was also in a playful mood in composing the lyric, incorporating a punning line about 'the bars where the stars drink tequila and wine (whine?)'. The song featured in Barclay James Harvest live sets for many years thereafter, and Les's fondness for it saw it reintroduced into his own band's live shows from 2007 onwards. A live version from the massive free concert in Berlin in August 1980 was used as the B-side of the band's 1983 single, 'Just A Day Away'.

'Capricorn' (John Lees)

'Capricorn' fuelled much speculation about the meaning of its portentous lyrics, all dashed when John revealed that they were actually cut up titles or phrases from some of his favourite books, à la 'Nova Lepidoptera'. In a 1989 interview for fan club magazine *Nova Lepidoptera*, John explained:

> I've written quite a few songs like that – that's a particular type of writing that David Bowie I know uses a lot, as well. What you do, basically, is you write all these things down as a list, then you cut them all up as sentences or even words, and you mix them all and jumble them all up, then you pull them out and fit them together.

Forty years on, John can't recall which books featured, but it's possible to detect fragments from the works of Edmund Spenser, Terence Rattigan and

L.P. Hartley among others. Whatever their origin, there's no denying that they are combined in such a way to produce some beautifully evocative imagery. It may also be germane to the debate to note that John himself is, astrologically speaking, a Capricorn. An edit of the song was released as the second single from the album in Britain and Germany in March 1980, to coincide with a European tour, but didn't make the charts.

'Play To The World' (Les Holroyd)

'Play To The World', Les's much-loved closer, sees the album out in fine style. The piece leads off with some almost classical-sounding synth parts, played by Les himself. They are followed by John's spacey lead guitar runs and Les's insistent piano, before the song builds into a big power ballad, topped off by a sax solo played by Alan Fawkes (keeping it in the family, Alan had previously worked with Steve Broomhead – by now part of Woolly Wolstenholme's new band, Mæstoso – on a Tim Hart album produced by David Rohl). With Barclay James Harvest breaking live attendance records and attracting an ever-increasing, adoring public in spite of Woolly's absence, it must have seemed as though they really were playing to the world.

Turn Of The Tide (1981)

Personnel:
John Lees: guitars and vocals
Les Holroyd: guitars, bass, keyboards and vocals
Mel Pritchard: drums and percussion
Kevin McAlea: keyboards, saxophone
Colin Browne: keyboards, guitar, bass and backing vocals
Recorded at Marcus Music, Kensington, London, September 1980 to March 1981 (except for 'Life Is For Living', which was recorded at Polygram Studios on 12 September 1980)
Producer: Barclay James Harvest and Martin Lawrence
Engineer: Martin Lawrence, assisted by Liz Biddiscombe
Record Label: Polydor
UK release date: May 1981
Highest chart places: UK: 55, Germany: 2, Switzerland: 1, France: 10, Norway: 4

Striking while the iron was hot, within a fortnight of the biggest gig in Barclay James Harvest's entire history, at which they had played to an estimated audience of anything up to a quarter of a million people, the band were at Polygram Studios in London, recording a new single. The fan club newsletter announced that this would be a double A-side of the two new songs premiered in Berlin: 'In Memory Of The Martyrs' and 'Life Is For Living'. In the event, it was decided not to use 'In Memory Of The Martyrs', possibly because it was too long, but instead to go with Les's song as the sole A-side. By the time the single was released in November, the band had already begun work on their next album, this time at Marcus Music Studios in London's Bayswater. *Turn Of The Tide* marked a number of major changes for the band. It was the first album to be recorded without any initial input from Woolly (although his presence lingered on in at least one song – 'Death Of A City' had first been performed, albeit in a quite different form, back in 1967). The album was also the band's first digital recording, and their first for many years not to be recorded at Strawberry. One link remained with the studio, however, as Martin Lawrence, who had worked with BJH on *XII* and *Eyes Of The Universe*, was again co-opted as engineer and co-producer, assisted by Marcus Music in-house sound engineer, Liz Biddiscombe. Kevin McAlea and Colin Browne also provided continuity, having played with John, Les and Mel on the 1980 tour and at the Berlin concert. The set up in the studio was nothing if not lavish: Mel had five separate drum kits set up and was reported to be keen to buy another! There was no shortage of new songs, either: John told the German press that 'Les and I have written a lot of new songs; there's enough material for at least two LPs.' Ironically, now that the Barclays were without a full-time keyboard player, *Turn Of The Tide*, released in May 1981, became their most keyboard-orientated album to date.

In hindsight, the album marked a break with the BJH sound of old, its typical early eighties synthesiser overload setting the tone for much of the band's eighties output. The squeaky clean, rather clinical digital sound, generally leisurely tempo and unashamed pitch at a much more commercial market weren't to everyone's taste. The album is not generally regarded as one of the band's finest moments amongst UK fans, alienating some of the band's older followers and lovers of prog rock, but enjoys much greater popularity on the Continent, where it attracted a new generation of fans. In that it was undoubtedly a big success in achieving exactly what it set out to do. In Germany, with 'Life Is For Living' riding high in the singles chart, the album garnered sufficient advance orders to qualify for a gold disc before it was even released, and went straight into the chart at number 3. In France, it made number 10, in Norway number 4, while in Switzerland it did even better, entering at pole position. In the UK it reached a more modest position of number 55, but this was, at least, an improvement on its predecessor.

Sleeve Design

The album's art direction was again overseen by Polydor's Alwyn Clayden, but the cover design which illustrated the title so aptly was by Bob Carlos Clarke, an up and coming Irish-born photographer. Clarke would go on to achieve fame and notoriety for his portraits and erotica. The front and reverse of the single sleeve are mirror images, both literally and metaphorically, showing a parched cityscape shimmering in a heat haze on the front, and the same landscape reversed on the back, now flooded and with heavy storm clouds above. Beautiful and memorable imagery, embellished with the by now obligatory Barclay James Harvest butterfly, resulted in one of the band's most attractive album sleeves.

'Waiting On The Borderline' (Les Holroyd)

An electronic keyboard riff and synth bass set the tone for the album on the opening track, a Les Holroyd song about the hurt and recriminations surrounding the end of a relationship. The repetitive rhythm and the keyboards provided by guest musician Kevin McAlea give the song a hypnotic aura, but it's noticeable that there's little or no contribution from John on the recording. If the first album the band recorded as a trio, *Eyes Of The Universe,* had been a step away from the old organic, Mellotron-washed seventies sound, then *Turn Of The Tide* marked a sea change, with digital instruments and recording techniques to the forefront in the first BJH recordings of the eighties. The gaps between Les's and John's styles were becoming more noticeable. 'Waiting On The Borderline' was issued as a promo-only single for radio play by Polydor France, backed with another Holroyd composition from the album, 'Echoes And Shadows', but made little impact.

'How Do You Feel Now?' (John Lees)

Kevin McAlea's piano introduces one of John Lees' most personal, autobiographical songs, written in celebration of the birth of his first child, Esther, in July 1980 – just a month before the free concert in Berlin (which became the first gig she ever attended!). Addressed to John's wife, Olwen, the lyrics, affecting in their simplicity, reflect the importance John has always placed on family, and his yearning to become a father. The sentiments made the song very special to John, even though he is on record as saying that somebody else should have sung it:

> I really think that I was too personally involved with 'How Do You Feel Now' to do the song justice vocally. I would like to hear someone do a cover version.

The saxophone solo was played by Kevin McAlea, now a regular guest musician on BJH recordings and live shows.

'Back To The Wall' (Les Holroyd)

More synthesizers and a trademark bassline herald Les's next contribution, partly inspired by the situation in Berlin and the band's free concert there. The lyric reflects both the plight of the East Berliners, 'waiting on the other side', and the band members' own experience at the show, where they literally had their backs to the Berlin Wall. The lyric also supplies the album title: 'He's been waiting on the other side / He's been waiting for the turn of the tide'.

The recording is notable for Mel Pritchard's first use of electronic drums, as he told the band's fan club:

> If a song or an arrangement requires the use of electronic percussion, I have no real problems in adapting to their use. For example, on the track 'Back To The Wall' I used a computerised drum machine called a LinnDrum.

'Highway For Fools' (John Lees)

Back to some heavy-riffing lead guitar now, with a no-nonsense rocker attacking the 'diamond love' mercenary approach of certain quarters of the music business and its emphasis on the pursuit of money over artistic integrity. John makes his point with the lyrically punning 'that kind of rock don't appeal' – he was uneasy about the price the band might have to pay for increasing commercial success, and Woolly Wolstenholme's departure seems to have occasioned some soul-searching on John's part, too.

'Echoes And Shadows' (Les Holroyd)

This is a beautifully atmospheric work and a thoroughbred ballad from the same stable as 'Play To The World'. The evocative, mystical lyrics are apparently about a love affair, although they could equally be interpreted as a reflection on the impermanence of material things. That may be to read too much into the words, though, since Les himself has always placed more emphasis on melody than lyrics:

> When I write a song, most of the time the music or riff comes first. I work on the principle of concerts – more often than not you cannot hear the lyrics the first time you hear a song, so, initially, the music and melody are more important to me.

For the recording, very little was played live, as Mel explained:

> Sometimes I lay down a rough rhythm track – we call this a click track – and we used this on 'Echoes And Shadows'. The track is then slowly rebuilt with completely new instrumentation. Consequently, tracks like that aren't rehearsed in themselves, except as an arrangement. Other tracks like 'Doctor Doctor' are played and recorded live, and normal overdubs (voices, percussion, guitar etc.) added.

'Death Of A City' (John Lees)

This song is a real throwback, having originally been written in a very different form way back in 1967. The band had recorded demo versions of it at Intercity Sound in Stockport, and at Decca's studios when that label expressed an interest in signing the fledgeling band, but then the song was shelved for more than a decade. John decided to revive it, re-writing all the verses and adding a driving guitar riff, whilst the slower choruses are lifted directly from the original. Several of John's songs composed in that early period share a similar apocalyptic theme of destruction, and it's no accident that one of the new lines refers to 'after the day'.

'I'm Like A Train' (Les Holroyd)

By way of contrast, Les pitches in with one of the album's brighter, piano-led songs, describing the start of a love affair and the radical changes in lifestyle that it brings. 'I'm Like A Train' includes some lyrical fragments suggested by Mel Pritchard when Les was short on inspiration. Not generally known as a songwriter, Mel nevertheless made some important contributions to some of Les's songs, and in one interview gave an interesting insight into his role:

> In the past, I've helped with Les and his lyrics. When it comes to the time for the next album, I usually have just a few pages of ideas, words that are thrown together, and he picks up on that.

'Doctor Doctor' (John Lees)

One of the advantages of digital recording is that, whilst it occasionally sounds rather clinical, it allows for increased separation and dynamic range. That's exemplified on this track, where certain parts leap out of the speakers, notably the rather fine 'plucked' bass playing on this track. The song extols the virtues of love as 'a natural panacea', but also offers an insight into the depression from which John had been suffering at the time, and the struggles he went through during his withdrawal from prescription anti-depressants.

'Life Is For Living' (Les Holroyd)

Fresh from its triumphant live debut at the Berlin concert, 'Life Is For Living', with its catchy tune and clap-along chorus, was a huge hit even before the band had finished recording the album. It entered the German chart at the end of

December 1980, eventually climbing to number 2. In Switzerland, it went one better, providing the band with their first-ever chart-topping record by reaching number 1 on 1 March 1981 and remaining at the top for four weeks. Even in the UK, where the band was, by now, deeply unfashionable, the single received some airplay, and made the Top 75 – possibly helped by a special promotional single issued to radio stations which featured an enthusiastic advertising voiceover from long-time BJH fan and BBC Radio One DJ, Alan 'Fluff' Freeman. For the album release, the song was remixed, and some extra vocal and keyboard parts were added. Both versions are included on the Esoteric label remasters of the album.

'In Memory Of The Martyrs' (John Lees)

The other song premiered at the free concert in Berlin was John's 'In Memory Of The Martyrs', a poignant and beautiful lament for those who lost their lives attempting to cross the Berlin Wall. In the album credits, John dedicated it to Philip John Ireland:

> … My cousin, who was tragically killed on the roads in West Germany while I was recording the LP. It was a sad waste of a young and much-loved person. He seemed to have a common ground with the young people who were killed in trying to make their escape from East to West Berlin.

In recent times the song has enjoyed a new lease of life, received with great acclaim at John Lees' Barclay James Harvest live performances from 2016 onwards, including a bucket-list-fulfilling appearance for the band members at that year's Glastonbury Festival.

Related Song:
'Shades Of B Hill' (John Lees)

When it was decided that 'In Memory Of The Martyrs' would be too long to be used as a double A-side single with 'Life Is For Living', a new B-side was required. In the UK, France and The Netherlands that took the form of this John Lees composition, a song which would not appear on the album, thereby enhancing the appeal of the single to collectors. Something of a departure from John's and BJH's normal style, it's a 'crooner', which the band recorded in downtime at Strawberry Studios as a tongue in cheek mickey-take, not planning on it ever being released! The enigmatic title could be taken as a reference to the Fats Domino's classic, 'Blueberry Hill', but the actual origins of it are lost in the mists of time. The German record company elected to use 'Sperratus' from *Eyes Of The Universe* as the B-side for their single of 'Life Is For Living' instead. The result was that 'Shades Of B Hill' remained largely unknown in Germany until it appeared on the *Alone We Fly* rarities compilation CD in 1990, and subsequently as a bonus track on remastered versions of *Turn Of The Tide*.

Ring Of Changes (1983)

Personnel:
John Lees: guitars and vocals
Les Holroyd: bass and vocals
Mel Pritchard: drums and percussion
Bias Boshell: keyboards
Kevin McAlea: keyboards on 'Midnight Drug'
New World Philharmonic Orchestra: orchestration on 'Paraiso Dos Cavalos' and 'Fifties Child'
Conductor: David Katz
Orchestral arrangements: Pip Williams
Henry Morris: backing vocals
Recorded at Far Studios, Frankfurt, January to March 1983
Mixed at RAK Studios, London
Producer: Pip Williams
Engineer: Gregg Jackman, assisted by Chris Dickie
Mastering Engineer: Melvyn Abrahams at Strawberry Mastering, London
Record Label: Polydor
UK release date: 16 May 1983
Highest chart places: UK: 36, Germany: 4, Switzerland: 2

By the end of 1982, Barclay James Harvest were enjoying their greatest commercial success to date; the live album, *Berlin – A Concert For The People* had topped the charts in Germany, shipping more than a quarter of a million copies by the day of release, and the band had toured extensively in Germany and France, playing to a total audience of well over half a million in 1982 alone. The producer selected for their next studio album was Pip Williams, one-time member of Eurovision hopefuls Bardot, and whose credits included The Moody Blues' *Long Distance Voyager* and Status Quo's *Whatever You Want* and *Rocking All Over The World.* It was decided to record the album in Germany, as Williams explained:

> We used Far studios, which belong to Frank Farian, the producer of Boney M, in Frankfurt. The group was having a year out of the country for tax purposes, and Far was the only studio that had all the digital gear as well as all the backup analogue equipment we wanted.

Williams was enthusiastic about digital recording, and also saw a marketing opportunity:

> The idea to record the album digitally for a CD version came about because we saw we could have a first with the simultaneous release of a new LP, Compact Disc and Cassette, the three main formats.

The studio had just opened, and the state-of-the-art digital recording gear was so new that nobody seemed to know how it worked! Mel Pritchard told German magazine *Bravo* magazine in late November 1982:

> In the last few months, we had terrible trouble in Germany with Frank Farian's new recording studio, where we want to record our new album. A great studio with all the trimmings, but apparently nobody can work it! We had to stop again and again because the echoes weren't right, or there was nothing at all on the tape. Not a single song is finished.

The recording sessions were abandoned and the planned release date put back to 1983, whilst the band rehearsed for the second half of a European Tour which kept them on the road from late October to the beginning of December. January 1983 saw recording get underway in earnest, with the teething troubles now resolved. A new face for these sessions was keyboardist Tobias 'Bias' Boshell, former member of folk/rock band Trees and the writer of 'I've Got The Music In Me', Kiki Dee's big hit from 1974. It was whilst working on Kiki's *Perfect Timing* album that he met Pip, who thought that he would be a good fit for BJH, too. Henry B. Morris, who is credited with 'occasional backing vocals', was a member of seventies bands Squaw and Palomino, and was Pip Williams' assistant for several years through the Moodies/Bardot period. Pip's remit was to give the band a more commercial, Stateside radio-friendly sound, in the same way that he had done for The Moodies and Quo. He achieved this by taking on some of the arrangements himself, in particular orchestrating two of John's songs, 'Fifties Child' and 'Paraiso Dos Cavalos'. The use of real strings (The New World Philharmonic Orchestra conducted by David Katz) represented a nod to the band's history, but with lush, honeyed arrangements more suited to the eighties marketplace. Pip was assisted by Gregg Jackman, who had also been the engineer on *Long Distance Voyager*. With the album finally completed in March 1983, Polydor pulled out all the stops for the release of *Ring Of Changes*, aware of the band's massive popularity on the Continent, and hopeful that their success could be replicated at home, too. Lavish launch parties were held for the world's press in a castle in Hamburg, in Paris (halfway up the Eiffel Tower!) and on board *The Elizabethan,* a replica of an 1890s Mississippi paddle steamer, on a cruise on the River Thames in London with DJ and long-time Barclays fan Alan Freeman. The London launch even received some very welcome coverage on daytime Radio One! The publicity paid off: the album went straight into the charts at number 4 in Germany and number 2 in Switzerland, and even made the UK Top 40, peaking at number 36. It was well-received by fans at the time, particularly on the Continent, and it's a homogenous, consistent piece of work, which has worn better than some of the band's other eighties output.

Sleeve Design

The concept and design for the cover were a joint effort between Polydor's Alwyn Clayden and BJH's manager, David Walker. The album title was intended to reflect what would be a year of change for BJH, living in Germany and recording there for the first time, with a change in producer and working with new musicians. In keeping with the big-budget for recording and promotion, the vinyl LP version of *Ring Of Changes* sported a gatefold sleeve with a die-cut circle on the front, through which could be seen a stylised atom design, complete with BJH butterfly. The title and the handwritten lyrics are arranged in rings around the cut-out circle – aesthetically pleasing, although it has the unfortunate side-effect of making them rather difficult to read! Photography for the sleeve was by Tony Latham, Alwyn Clayden, and Bob Norris, including tiny insets of John, Les and Mel's faces in the skies above the futuristic landscape on the back of the cover.

'Fifties Child' (John Lees)

The first thing the listener to the *Ring Of Changes* album hears is real strings, performing an orchestral précis of some of the album's musical themes, before the band plunge into 'Fifties Child'. One of the strongest songs on the album, this John Lees number laments the lost idealism of those who grew up in the sixties and seventies and espouses a return to the old ideals of peace and love. It's a lovely, acoustic-led clarion call for an alternative to the conspicuous consumption and dog-eat-dog culture which seemed to be the dominant values of 1980s Britain. The orchestral parts of the album were recorded completely separately, back in London. Sound engineer Gregg Jackman told *Electronics and Music Maker* magazine:

> In the initial stages, Pip was presented with a batch of demos and we just did what we felt was right for each song, but since the new technology was there, we felt it was time to use it. The exception to this was the orchestra which appears on a couple of songs. They were recorded at RAK on analogue 16 track with an SMPTE code.

The code to which Gregg referred is an electronic standard used to timestamp the tapes so that they could then be married up precisely with the digital recordings of the band. 'Fifties Child', *sans* orchestra, made a return to the live arena when it was included in John Lees' Barclay James Harvest live sets from 2012 on, where it was greeted like a long-lost old friend.

'Looking From the Outside' (Les Holroyd)

Les Holroyd's first contribution to the album is 'Looking From The Outside', a strongly melodic mid-paced song dealing with alienation. There's an ambiguity to the lyric, which at first listen seems to be about a relationship where the writer can't reach a partner on an emotional level, but then can also be read as the first recognition that all might not be well within the band. John Lees' and David Walker's later comments that this album would not have been made were it not for the strong character of Pip Williams holding the band together lend a degree of credibility to the latter interpretation. The keyboards used throughout the album are two Jupiter 8s and an Oberheim OBX 6-voice, played by Bias Boshell, described by Pip Williams as 'the best keyboard player about at the moment, although he's not really part of the BJH "family unit"'. The unusual bass sound was courtesy of a Roland Bass Guitar synth.

'Teenage Heart' (John Lees)

In 'Teenage Heart' John revisits his youth and recalls the agonies of young love and pubescent angst. Like most of John's songs, it was written on guitar:

> Although a lot of the album is keyboard-based, I write mainly on guitar and play a little guitar synth. During recording, I used The Paul, an inexpensive version of the Gibson Les Paul with basic facilities and finish which was released in a limited edition a couple of years ago.

'High Wire' (Les Holroyd)

The band come closest to rocking out on 'High Wire', in which a driving beat underscores the tale of a precariously unbalanced relationship where the protagonist is badly-treated and predicts that his lover will come to a bad end, but can't resist coming back for more. Like much of the album, it's a synth-heavy recording, and the drumming is predominantly on a Simmons electronic kit, as popularised by Spandau Ballet in the early eighties. Pip Williams described the percussion set up thus:

> The main kit is a Simmons all the way through until you get to the end, where the fills are played on an acoustic kit. This is the first time the band has used a Simmons, simply because there was one available in the studio. We also used the Linn LM-1 and LinnDrum for percussion, just for the congas and similar sounds and for keeping the sequences in strict tempo. We find click tracks a bit inhuman to work with, and Mel is good enough a drummer to play along to. In fact, there aren't any sequencers in use – just the arpeggiators of the Jupiter 8s – because sequencers really come from a different style of music.

'Midnight Drug' (John Lees)

The contrast between the natural highs of love and the artificiality of chemically-induced pleasure is not a new subject for John (*cf.* 'Hymn'), but 'Midnight Drug' is more personal. It was written about a particular friend whose lifestyle was giving John cause for concern. The arrangement is very unusual for Barclay James Harvest in that the lead vocals are shared, with Les to the fore on the middle eight before John picks up the tale again.

'Waiting For The Right Time' (Les Holroyd)

Next up is a typically lush Les Holroyd ballad. A hypnotic synthesised bass-line and multi-tracked backing vocals introduce 'Waiting For The Right Time', a bittersweet romance about loneliness after a heartbreak, with Les holding out the hope of a reconciliation and a happy ending. The song was chosen as the second single from the album in the UK, and released in seven-inch and twelve-inch formats. For the seven-inch version, the recording was shortened by means of a ham-fisted piece of editing which managed to destroy the time structure of the song. Legendary French songstress Françoise Hardy paid Les the compliment of recording her own French-language version of the song, as the title track to her 1988 album, *Décalages*, but declared herself, 'not too happy with my adaptation.'

'Just A Day Away (Forever Tomorrow)' (John Lees)

The release of the album was trailed by a single of 'Just A Day Away', released on 5 April in Germany and 9 May in the UK, backed with 'Rock 'N' Roll Lady' recorded live at the 1980 Berlin concert. The British single was boosted by the release of a shaped red and blue picture disc cut in the form of a butterfly, with 'Looking From The Outside' from the same album billed as the B-side, helping the single to reach number 68 in the UK chart. A breakdown in communication between the record company and the pressing plant resulted in the initial batch of picture disc singles being pressed with the B-side of the standard black vinyl seven-inch single. The error was corrected for later pressings, but such a large batch had already been manufactured that the 'correct' version is now sought after by collectors! In Germany, even without the aid of gimmicks, the single reached number 40, whilst in Switzerland, it made the top five. It's a pleasant enough love song, but the arrangement does it few favours, with a rather unconvincing mariachi-style 'trumpet' solo and a syrupy synthesised string arrangement. The single was supported by a promo video featuring the band dressed as convicts on a chain gang, wielding pick-axes under the watchful eye of a mysterious oriental female guard and a black obelisk which could have come straight out of *2001 – A Space Odyssey*.

'Paraiso Dos Cavalos' (John Lees)

'Paraiso Dos Cavalos' is a musical recollection of a holiday which John and his family had recently enjoyed in Portugal. The 'Paradise Of The Horses' of the title was a riding club in the Quinta do Lago area of the Algarve, and Nico, Limpopo, Ipaminandas and Young Nero were the names of some of the horses they rode during their stay. It's a lovely song which effortlessly evokes long days of 'summer sunshine and cool green wine'. The gorgeous harp and real strings give the song a romantic flavour which complements the evocative descriptions of 'galloping on in the breaking waves' with 'the wind in your hair'. John's acoustic guitar is understated, because, as he put it:

> A lot of the guitar work is acoustic, it's a nice texture and it works well with synths. I want to work on a guitar sound to suit a particular song, not just to play flash solos that distract from the song itself. I'll do a solo if the song calls for it, but there aren't a lot of solos on Ring of Changes.

Fan club members voted 'Paraiso Dos Cavalos' their favourite song from the album shortly after its release, and it has stood the test of time well, making a welcome return to live performance with John Lees' Barclay James Harvest in 2016.

'Ring Of Changes' (Les Holroyd)

Morse code spells out 'ring of changes' to introduce Les's title track, reflecting John's love of amateur radio, a hobby he shared with his father. Unusually, the song was far from complete when recording began; Pip Williams recalled that 'The title track was a little unusual in that it started very simply and we kept adding to it with synthesiser sounds and electronic percussion.', and John described how 'it evolved from start to finish in the studio without being planned too much in advance.' The lyrics observe how everything and yet nothing changes, and Barclay James Harvest Featuring Les Holroyd, appropriately enough, still perform the song live today. The reprise of the orchestral theme at the end continues the album's circular *leitmotiv*, and brings us neatly back to where we came in. At one point it was planned to issue 'Ring Of Changes' as the second single from the album, and since the original version clocked in at well over seven minutes, it was edited down to four and a half minutes and remixed for radio, with a release date of 15 July scheduled for most European territories. At that point, though, Polydor's offices in the UK, France and Spain broke ranks, deciding to issue 'Waiting For The Right Time' instead, leaving Germany as the only country to stick with the original plan and issue the title track. The single duly appeared, initially in a picture sleeve featuring a less than flattering black and white photo of the band. This was swiftly withdrawn and replaced by the more attractive colour photo which was used for the 'Waiting For The Right Time' singles released elsewhere, making the original issue one of the band's most sought after collectables!

Related Song:

'Blow Me Down' (John Lees/Mel Pritchard)

Both singles featured the same flip side, John and Mel's previously unreleased 'Blow Me Down', an out-take from the album sessions and a rare collaboration: John asked Mel to come up with a favourite drum pattern around which to base a song. Those familiar with early seventies British rock and blues may recognise the musical quote which John included from Mel's song of choice: the 'ooh, la-la-la-yeah' refrain in the middle eight is a nod to Free's 'Heartbreaker'. Total anoraks may like to note that the German and Spanish singles included a count-in at the beginning of the B-side, which was absent from the UK cut – another collectors' item in the making!

Victims Of Circumstance (1984)

Personnel:
John Lees: guitars and vocals
Les Holroyd: bass, keyboards and vocals
Mel Pritchard: drums and percussion
Bias Boshell: keyboards
Joy Yates, Stevie Lange and Vicki Brown: backing vocals
Frank Ricotti: percussion
Strings: David Katz
Orchestral arrangements: Pip Williams
Recorded at Wisseloord Studios, Hilversum, Holland, September 1983 to January 1984
Mixed at Advision Studios, London; mastered at The Town House, London
Producer: Pip Williams
Engineer: Gregg Jackman
Assistant Engineer and Digital Assembly: David Jacob
Digital Mastering Engineer: Ian Cooper
Record Label: Polydor
UK release date: April 1984
Highest chart places: UK: 33, Germany: 4, France: 1, Switzerland: 1

In August 1983, John told *Electronics and Music Maker* magazine that 'We already have the songs written for the next album, and the other guys will be going to work on it soon. We won't tour until next year.' The recording studio chosen this time was in The Netherlands: Wisseloord Studios in Hilversum, founded by Philips in 1978 for the use of PolyGram artists. The line-up for the sessions was almost unchanged, with Pip Williams producing, Gregg Jackman as engineer and Bias Boshell guesting on keyboards. Pip was again responsible for the orchestral arrangements, which were performed by the David Katz Strings. There was one completely new aspect to this project, however, as for the first time in their career, the Barclays would employ three female backing singers: Stevie Lange (a respected session singer who had two American top twenty hits with a band called Night, and was married to record producer Mutt Lange), Vicki Brown (a member of The Vernons Girls and the first wife of fellow musician Joe Brown and mother of Sam Brown) and Joy Yates (a New Zealand-born singer who had worked with everyone from Cliff Richard to Monty Python). Sam Brown would take on her mother's role as a backing singer on subsequent live dates, together with her friend Jan Ince (herself replaced by another friend, Helen Chapelle, at the autumn shows for which Jan was not available). Initially, the intention was to have the backing singers perform on one song on the album, but they ended up singing on much of the record. John explained why:

> When you've got that many albums in the marketplace, you need to be looking for something different all the time, and it was felt that the girl singers would

complement some of the things we were doing. When we actually brought them in it was great and so we're even gonna take it a stage further now.

Les agreed:

We're trying to bring new people into the band and new ideas, and that's why the albums are selling so well.

Another new face was the vibraphonist and percussionist Frank Ricotti, who provided some additional percussion for the album. Recording began in September 1983, and the band found it hard work: Pip Williams insisted that all of the musicians turned up at ten a.m. every day, and he demanded discipline. John told German teen magazine *Popcorn*, 'There is hardly a day where we get out of the studio before midnight!' Recording was completed in January 1984, and the release of the album was preceded by a single of the title track, 'Victims Of Circumstance', on 16 March. The single became a surprise hit in France, where they had enjoyed relatively limited success previously, and went to number 1. When the album followed at the beginning of April, it emulated the single's chart-topping success in France, and, like *Ring Of Changes*, made number 4 in Germany. Even in the UK, it performed respectably well, making number 33, although older fans were less enamoured with the poppier style and the female backing vocals. The album divides fans to this day, and it's certainly a child of its time, with very eighties production values. Nevertheless, there are still some strong songs beneath the arrangements, as more recent live renditions by both current bands have demonstrated.

Sleeve Design

The album title and the very striking album sleeve were decided before recording began: the band's managers and record company art director Mike McCraith commissioned an art agency called Cream to design some album covers. The artist, Ian Kay, came up with an old poster for a Berlin *bierkeller* cabaret and the title *Victim Of Circumstance*. John was already familiar with the poster, painted by the famous illustrator Jo Steiner in 1912, as it was included in a book of old posters that he owned. The model was Senta Söneland, a famous actress of the day, who later committed suicide. John told the Friends Of Barclay James Harvest fan club in March 1985:

Strangely enough, I had written a song ('Rebel Woman') when the Korean 'plane was shot down by the Russians and the chorus was 'Victims of circumstance'. It was funny because I hadn't mentioned this and then this guy came up with it. Then Les wrote a song around the title.

A tear was added to the eye of the portrait, which resembles a nightmare-ish clown. As John put it:

With that we want to express that, basically, we're all clowns, we laugh when

> we feel like crying and we cry when we could laugh instead. We're all victims of circumstance.

Rather like the content of the album, the sleeve proved contentious: some applauded the bold and striking illustration, whilst others were appalled at how far the design was removed from the band's more pastoral imagery of the seventies. Even the band's iconic symbol seemed to have been added as a sop to tradition, in such a stylised form that it was barely recognisable as a butterfly – in fact, closer inspection reveals that it can also be seen as a representation of the theatrical masks of tragedy and comedy, cleverly reinforcing the theme of the album.

'Sideshow' (John Lees)

Pip Williams' production and orchestral arrangements make this album and *Ring Of Changes* very much a pair both sonically and in terms of their AOR sensibilities. The opening song, 'Sideshow', underlines the point, bearing a musical resemblance to 'Fifties Child' from the album's predecessor. Here, though, the string arrangement is reinforced by the female singers, and John and Les share the lead vocals. John revealed his thinking behind the song to rock magazine *Kerrang!* thus:

> I like to write songs with a little depth to them, yet which can still be appreciated on the most superficial of levels. The lyrics, if you study them, talk about how the media concentrates so much on the bad events that occur in the world. You rarely get anything positive being screened. Turning on the TV sometimes reduces me to tears, seeing the way man treats his fellow men.

It's sung not so much in anger, but rather as a lament for lost innocence, and, like 'Fifties Child', has been reintroduced into live performances by John Lees' Barclay James Harvest since 2012.

'Hold On' (Les Holroyd)

The tempo increases with 'Hold On', one of Les's rockier songs which became a staple of live sets, capturing the atmosphere of frenetic nightlife and club culture. A trademark John Lees lead guitar riff leads into the driving rhythm of the verse and a catchy chorus has the female backing singers to the fore. A quieter centre section highlights the talents of Bias Boshell on keyboards – on this album he played a Yamaha DX7, a Roland JP8 and a JX3, plus a Steinway grand piano.

'Rebel Woman' (John Lees)

Not, as some fans speculated at the time, a critique of Margaret Thatcher! The subject was actually Mother Russia in the days before *glasnost* and *perestroika* and the collapse of the Communist system, and John wrote the song following the shooting down of KAL007, the Korean Air Lines Boeing 747, by a Soviet Su-15 interceptor on 1 September 1983, killing all 269 passengers and crew aboard. The airliner was en route from Anchorage to Seoul, but deviated from its original planned route and flew through Soviet prohibited airspace, and was possibly mistaken by the Soviet Air Forces for an intruding U.S. spy plane. Here the brooding guitars and angry lyrics work well, but the arrangement around them still feels a little lightweight for the subject matter.

'Say You'll Stay' (Les Holroyd)

After the heavy main course, a gossamer confection in the form of an escapist love song from Les, conjuring a dream-world of romantic fantasy. The song also contains something of a lyrical barb with a side-swipe against the 'little people' who tell him what to do. A reference to some of the savage criticism which the band frequently had to endure from the music press, perhaps?

'For Your Love' (John Lees)

Fans got their first sneak preview of the contents of the album in the form of a Christmas message from John in the Friends Of Barclay James Harvest fan club newsletter:

> Light up the flame of love
> Whenever fear and darkness surround you.
> For only, with all our flames
> Joined together in one great light
> Can we hold back the cold night
> And bring peace to all mankind

'Light up the flame of love' is a direct quote from one of John's new songs, 'For Your Love', but it's not a conventional love song, as he later explained:

> 'For Your Love' is about the kids who hold up lighters at the end of our concerts. When I used to get depressed and feel nobody cared, I used to think of those kids who must really like the music. In the darkest moments of everyone's life, if they could just hold a flame up and everyone else did it too, it might force all the black and dark to go away. I went back to being a hippy for a split second!

A torch song, then?! In live performances on the 1984 tour to promote the album, the piece was slowed down and given room to breathe and came across much more powerfully as a result. 'Let it shine', sang John, and it did. An example of the live version can be found on the expanded, remastered Esoteric label set of *Victims Of Circumstance*, which includes the audio recordings of eleven songs originally released on a VHS video of the band's biggest-ever headlining UK show, at London's Wembley Arena.

'Victims Of Circumstance' (Les Holroyd)

The second side of the vinyl LP opens with a complete change of mood. This is an anti-war song, with some very bitter words for the politicians and leaders who keep their people in the dark and ignore their wishes. The lyrics are set to a deceptively innocuous melody and lightweight arrangement highlighting the female backing vocals and Pip Williams' Spanish guitar fills. Speaking on a Berlin radio station, Les told the young interviewers:

> I'm not a lyricist, you know, I don't write the lyrics to the song first, before the music. Just this once, I had the idea of writing something like 'Victims Of Circumstance'. I really felt let down by the situation in Europe and I realised how little we can do about it. The people elect the politicians so that they act in their interests, and then things happen that the majority of people didn't actually want, which I think is very unfair, and it's something that's going to affect not only our generation, but generations to come.

A promotional video for the single release of 'Victims Of Circumstance', directed by Keith MacMillan, depicted a nightmare society (well, it *was* shot in Fulham!) of zombies blindly following their leaders. Hope is not lost, though, as at the end a child stops the doomsday clock at one minute to midnight. The seven-inch and twelve-inch single formats used remixed instrumental versions of the song on the flip side, which are included on later CD issues.

'Inside My Nightmare' (John Lees)

The genesis of the next song was a road accident in John's local area:

> 'Inside My Nightmare' is a very tragic story that happened near to where I live. Some young kids were driving a car, just out for a ride, and missed a corner. Three of them walked away and one was killed. They were very young and it really affected me. I kept thinking, what if I'd just taken my girlfriend out for a drive and that happened to me at that age?'

John's manic vision of the aftermath of the tragedy is, perhaps, undermined somewhat by the pop sensibilities and over-enthusiastic use of the backing vocalists in the arrangement, but it remains a thought-provoking piece.

'Watching You' (Les Holroyd)

Pop sounds and ersatz reggae rhythms underscore a song which could be about the beginning of a relationship or a more disturbing kind of voyeurism. In either case, the writer is very wary, preferring to play a watching and waiting game before making any kind of commitment. Synth bass dominates the rhythm, whilst John's lead guitar licks offer an interesting contrast to Bias Boshell's contemporary keyboard sounds.

'I've Got A Feeling' (Les Holroyd)

The album closes with another Holroyd song, a languorous and wistful ballad about a parting from a loved one. The song was remixed and some saxophone parts added when it was lifted as the second single from the album. The seven-inch single was an edited version, but for some strange reason the full-length twelve-inch was only pressed up for promotional use in the UK, and wasn't made commercially available – except in France! This long version was later made available on *The Compact Story Of Barclay James Harvest* compilation, and on CD reissues of the *Victims Of Circumstance* album, whilst the seven-inch edit of the new recording (as well as the seven-inch instrumental version of the title track) were included on the 1996 rarities collection, *Endless Dream*.

Face To Face (1987)

Personnel:
John Lees: guitars and vocals
Les Holroyd: bass, keyboards and vocals
Mel Pritchard: drums and percussion
Kevin McAlea, Bias Boshell and Wix: additional keyboards
Andrew Jackman: writing and performance of string arrangement on 'Guitar Blues'
Frank Ricotti: additional percussion
Dick Morrissey: tenor saxophone on 'All My Life'
George Chandler, Richard Jon Smith, Jimmy Chambers, Lee Vanderbilt, Bill Fredericks and Jimmy Thomas: additional backing vocals on 'African'
Recorded at Friarmere Studios, Delph, Autumn 1986. Additional keyboard and percussion overdubs added at Chipping Norton Studios
Mixed at Mayfair Studios and Advision Studios, London; mastered by Mike Walker at Trident Studios
Producer: Barclay James Harvest and Gregg Jackman, except for 'Prisoner Of Your Love', 'Turn The Key', African', 'Following Me', 'All My Life' and 'Kiev', which were produced by Pip Williams, Gregg Jackman and Barclay James Harvest.
Engineer: Gregg Jackman, assisted by David Bland
Record Label: Polydor
UK release date: 30 January 1987
Highest chart places: UK: 65, Germany: 9, Switzerland: 7

Background

Whilst 1984's *Victims Of Circumstance* had been a commercial success, particularly in France, the band members felt that the experiment with a poppier sound and female backing vocalists for the album and associated tour had gone too far, and were aware that it had alienated some of their core supporters. After a hiatus whilst they took some much-needed time out for themselves and considered their future direction, an agreement was reached on their next move: a back-to-the-roots album playing to Barclay James Harvest's traditional strengths, with the emphasis very much on strong songwriting, melody and harmony. New material was first demoed in September 1985, with the Friends Of Barclay James Harvest fan club announcing a planned release date for a new album in the spring of 1986. The venue for recording was John's own Friarmere Studios in an old vicarage in the village of Delph, which had been intended primarily for use as a rehearsal studio. However, when it was found that Pip Williams, first choice as producer for the new album, was busy working on another project, BJH decided to use the new studio to record the album, even though it would mean a return to analogue recording. Gregg Jackman, who had previously undertaken engineering work for the band, was drafted in to engineer and co-produce the album. Unused to the luxury of unlimited studio time, the band took their time over getting exactly what they wanted, but this was something of a double-edged sword: recording of the album, now with the working title *Elements*, seemed to go on forever. When a few tracks still didn't meet with the band's complete approval, some extra work was done with Pip Williams at Chipping Norton Studios, and it was over a year before the album was finally completed. Now titled *Face To Face*, the album was released in February 1987 and marked at least a partial return to a more familiar Barclays style. In retrospect *Face To Face* is generally regarded by fans as something of a mixed bag. John admitted to the band's fan club magazine in April 1989 that he had been surprised by this:

> We were terribly disappointed about the reaction to Face To Face; we'd made a conscious effort to go back and look at the catalogue that we'd produced over the years, to try and take something from that, and we didn't really get the kind of reaction we thought we would. I thought that Face To Face was a great album, I thought it really worked.

After a three year delay since the last studio album, though, it was not altogether surprising that media interest, even in Germany, had waned. Unfortunately, the young French fans who had sent *Victims Of Circumstance* to Number 1 proved to be a fickle audience, and the album didn't even chart in France. It made it to number 65 in Britain without the benefit of much in the way of publicity. The German audience proved more loyal than their media (which largely ignored the album), propelling the album into the Top 10 and earning the band another gold record.

Sleeve Design

The cover illustration was by Karl Lloyd of design agency Green Ink, who had also designed the sleeve for the previous year's Moody Blues album, *The Other Side Of Life*. The artwork featured a modernistic, androgynous face, with the trademark butterfly reduced to a tiny motif in the eye of the face. On the back of the sleeve, to the relief of older fans, the band were photographed by Andy Earl in casual clothes in the reassuringly familiar surroundings of Saddleworth Moor. Art direction was once again by Alwyn Clayden.

'Prisoner Of Your Love' (Les Holroyd)

Les kicks off the album with the very commercial 'Prisoner Of Your Love', starting with some typically eighties keyboard sounds and synthesised breathy backing vocals which could have fitted seamlessly onto *Victims Of Circumstance*. The song develops in more muscular vein when Mel's drums and John's guitar riffs take over the beat, and fades out with some Chicago-esque brass sounds. The song was premiered (together with 'He Said Love') on the *Peter's Pop Show* TV programme in Germany in December 1986, before the album came out, and may have been under consideration for release as a single.

'He Said Love' (John Lees)

The first single from the album was 'He Said Love', released in November 1986. It was BJH's most overtly Christian song to date, the lyric being basically a condensed version of the New Testament. John Lees told *Pop Rocky* magazine about the sentiments behind the song:

> My wife Olwen was pregnant again after three miscarriages. We then went to a specialist, who thought that she might have cancer and would have to have an operation. At that time, I just prayed like mad, and indeed my prayers were heard and everything went well. My wife didn't need the operation and had a healthy boy, so I wrote 'He Said Love' as a thank you.

Musically, the celebration of the birth of John and Olwen's second child (John Joseph, on 13 January 1986) bears a close family resemblance to 'Hymn', and, with its seasonal relevance, was an obvious choice for single release just before Christmas, but didn't chart. Keeping it in the family, the black and white promo video made in Portugal for the song by Clive Richardson Films features not just the band members looking suitably biblical on a fishing boat, but also includes a brief cameo from John's six-year old daughter, Esther, holding a pigeon.

'Alone In The Night' (John Lees)

There is a great contrast in this excellent contribution from John between the atmospheric, almost ethereal opening and the powerful guitar riffs which herald the chorus. It's a familiar theme of lost love and rejection, but a particularly memorable evocation of it, nonetheless. Amongst fans, it is regarded as one of the strongest songs on the album. Live performances were even more compelling, as captured on the *Glasnost* live album the following year.

'Turn The Key' (Les Holroyd)

An unashamedly poppy, lively song from the pen of Les, with a neat melody line played on the guitar and some synthesised choral vocals in the middle eight before a trademark key change. This track formed part of the 1987 live set and appeared on the *Glasnost* CD and cassette, but not on the LP and video versions.

'You Need Love' (John Lees) [on CD and MC only]

This song was missing from the vinyl version of the album – a pity, since John's bittersweet reflections on the difficulties of sustaining a long-term relationship after the first flush of romance arguably make for a stronger track than some which did make the cut for the LP.

'Kiev' (Les Holroyd)

The band's political consciousness remained intact: Les's 'Kiev' is a ballad drawing on the 'Whiter Shade Of Pale' musical template, drawing attention to the plight of all those affected by the Chernobyl disaster of April 1986, when an accident at a nuclear power station in the then Soviet Union killed many and contaminated a wide area of the Ukraine, close to Kiev.

'African' (John Lees)

This was, perhaps, John's most openly political song thus far; a personal view of African politics in general and an excoriating denunciation of the apartheid system in South Africa in particular (before white minority rule was finally replaced following the 1994 multiracial general election, in which Nelson Mandela led the ANC to victory and became president). It's a savage indictment of racism and exploitation, prompted by one particular incident, as John explained:

> 'African' was written off the back of that mining disaster where all those people were killed; it had to be literal, it had to be brutal.

The disaster in question happened on 16th September 1986, when 177 mineworkers were killed at Kinross Mine in one of South Africa's worst mining disasters. An acetylene tank sparked flames that swept through the mining tunnel igniting plastic covering on the wiring. The flames also set fire to polyurethane foam that is used to keep walls in the mine dry. The burning plastic combined with polyurethane and churned toxic fumes that filled the shafts, choking miners to death. South Africa's gold mines were notoriously dangerous workplaces for the country's mainly black miners – in the period between 1900 and 1993, 69,000 mineworkers died in accidents and more than one million were seriously injured. The backing vocalists on 'African' were George Chandler (lead singer of '70s funk band The Olympic Runners), Richard Jon Smith (a singer, songwriter and producer born in Cape Town), Jimmy Chambers (Trinidadian session singer who would later form the band Londonbeat with George Chandler and Jimmy Helms), Lee Vanderbilt (also from Trinidad, a singer and writer associated with the likes of Tina Charles, Elkie Brooks and Joan Armatrading), Bill Fredericks (The Drifters) and Jimmy Thomas (Arkansas-born soul singer who worked with Ike and Tina Turner).

'Following Me' (Les Holroyd)

A medium pace love song from Les which, like 'Life Is For Living', uses the metaphor of flight to conjure up a feeling of freedom and romance in the music. The pure pop of 'Following Me' sits rather uneasily after the outraged vehemence of 'African', and is one of the album's more lightweight moments.

'All My Life' (Les Holroyd)

A subtle bass line and delicate melody set the tone for Les's next contribution, the dreamy 'All My Life', before Mel's drum break clatters in and provides the setting for a tenor sax solo. The latter is courtesy of Dick Morrissey, the jazz-rock saxophonist probably best known for his work with the band If (which also included Dennis Elliott, later of King Crimson and Foreigner) in the early seventies. 'All My Life' was used as the B-side of the Germany-only single of 'Panic'.

'Panic' (John Lees)

The mood changes again with Les's ethereal ballad rudely followed by a tongue-in-cheek, uncharacteristically heavy rocker from John, about the relationship between fans and the music they love. A drastically remixed version, which many prefer to the original, was issued as a single in Germany only. The new interpretation was a great improvement on the rather lacklustre original; clever use of loops to extend the piece, combined with a much harder edge to the mix, suit the song well. Les explained why the band had moved away from their usual sound:

> We've always done up-tempo rock numbers in the past, but this time in the studio we had a little bit more time to experiment with sounds and voices and things, and we just tried on that particular number to see how far away we could get from the normal Barclay James Harvest sound into something that was a little more commercial. It was just an experiment, but it seems to have worked quite well.

In addition to the now-standard seven-inch and twelve-inch singles, 'Panic' was the band's first CD single release – clearly, Polydor's art department weren't familiar with this new-fangled format, as the cover design proclaims that it runs at 45 rpm.

'Guitar Blues' (John Lees)

The song which is regarded by many as a high point of this album wasn't actually a new composition, as John told the fan club:

> 'Guitar Blues', interesting song, that. It goes back a long way, it was written for Ring Of Changes. There were a couple that didn't get on that album and that was one of them, so it went on the Face To Face album.

In fact, there had been some debate about the advisability of doing a song with a Moody Blues-ish title (*cf.* The Blue Jays' 'Blue Guitar') on an album produced by Pip Williams, and the song was shelved. Fortunately, John revived it four years later, with a sumptuous string arrangement written and performed by Andrew Pryce Jackman. Andrew was the brother of Gregg and boasted an impressive musical pedigree. This included being a member of a band called Syn with Chris Squire and Pete Banks (pre-Yes); arranging and conducting Peter Skellern's 1972 hit 'You're A Lady'; becoming conductor of the London Symphony Orchestra and working on two Top 10 albums with Rush! The lyric of 'Guitar Blues' is ambiguous – it can be read as a lament for a lost lover, but it also makes sense as a tribute to the man who was closest to John in the original Barclay James Harvest, to wit Woolly Wolstenholme. Whatever the subject matter, the soaring strings and inspired guitar solo ensured its popularity, and it is widely regarded as a neglected BJH classic. In 2018 it received its first-ever live airing as part of an acoustic medley at a 50th Anniversary celebration of BJH music by John Lees' Barclay James Harvest.

'On The Wings Of Love' (Les Holroyd) [on CD only]
The closing track on the CD didn't even make it onto the LP or cassette versions of the album, which seems astonishing given the popularity of the song and its reception when the band performed it live. It did appear on the B-side of the seven-inch and twelve-inch singles of 'He Said Love', but that hardly justifies the omission of one of Les's strongest contributions from two formats of the album. It's the type of ballad in which Les specialises, a plaintive love song with shades of Chicago, Elton John and even 10cc, whilst remaining instantly recognisable as the incurably romantic side of BJH.

Welcome To The Show (1990)

Personnel:
John Lees: guitars and vocals
Les Holroyd: bass, guitars, keyboards and vocals
Mel Pritchard: drums and percussion
Richard Close: additional keyboards
Steve Pigott: additional keyboards
Ian Wilson: backing vocals
Steve Butler: backing vocals
Andy Hamilton: saxophone on 'Where Do We Go'
Michael Hehir: guitar
Jon Astley: Fairlight programming
Darrin Tidsey: assistance with Fairlight programming
Recorded at Revolution Studios, Cheadle Hulme, March to September 1989
Producer: Jon Astley and Andy MacPherson
Engineer: Andy MacPherson, additional engineering by Michael Haas
Record Label: Polydor
UK release date: 5 March 1990
Highest chart places: Germany: 10, Switzerland: 7

Following the slightly disappointing reception for 1987's *Face To Face* and the following year's live album, *Glasnost*, there was a sense within the Barclay James Harvest camp that they needed to re-establish an upward trajectory, and that making a very special album would be the best way to achieve that. In March 1989 work began to that end. In pursuit of a more contemporary sound, a new producer was drafted in: the brother-in-law of Pete Townshend, Jon Astley had previously produced albums by the likes of The Who, Eric Clapton and Sad Café, as well as releasing two excellent solo albums himself, *Everybody Loves The Pilot (Except The Crew)* and *The Compleat Angler*. Astley frequently worked with Andy MacPherson as a production team at Andy's own Revolution Studios in Cheadle Hulme, near Stockport, and this was the chosen venue for recording the new BJH album. The pair quickly established a rapport with the band, and Revolution's Fairlight sampler, of which Astley was a big fan, enabled the band to get the precise sounds that they wanted. That meant, though, that much of the recording was not 'live' in the traditional sense – Mel's drums, for instance, were simply sampled into the Fairlight and 'played' via the keyboard. Mel seemed satisfied with this way of working, and with the results, telling the fan club:

> The record company got Jon Astley and ourselves together, and we decided we wanted the classic Barclay James Harvest brought up to date, and I think it's worked.

A number of session musician friends of the production team were drafted in to produce particular sounds as required, including some familiar names from the local scene – old friend Ritchie Close contributed additional keyboards, Sad Café's Ian Wilson provided backing vocals and his bandmate Mike Hehir created some guitar sounds. Steve Butler (previously lead vocalist with Monroe) also sang backing vocals, while Steve Pigott of Living In A Box produced the dramatic keyboard effects in 'Lady Macbeth'. Veteran saxophonist Andy Hamilton also made a guest appearance. The first results of the recording sessions were impressive, and there was a real feeling around the band that this could, indeed, represent a renaissance for Barclay James Harvest. The UK record company began to invest more time and money in promotion, splashing out around £30,000 on a promotional video for lead single, 'Cheap The Bullet'. Their renewed interest created a buzz around the finished record, which had a diversity and freshness to it. The album was released in March 1990 and took its title from the Les Holroyd song, 'Welcome To The Show' – perhaps unwisely, since the casual browser might easily mistake it for a live album. Fortunately, as the band had hoped, the album was a strong one, inviting comparisons with earlier classics, whilst Jon Astley's and Andy MacPherson's input gave it a more contemporary sound. A number of television appearances to promote the German single release of the title track helped to propel the parent album into the Top 10 in Germany and Switzerland, and it went on to sell over 250,000 copies in Germany, qualifying it for a gold disc. Still regarded by some as their best work of the post-Wolstenholme era, *Welcome To The Show* brought Barclay James Harvest into the nineties in fine style.

Sleeve Design

The album artwork was created by Storm Thorgerson, the legendary designer best known for his work with Hipgnosis, and has echoes of his contemporaneous covers for Pink Floyd. Identically cloaked figures, faces hidden by mirrors, are dotted around the landscape of the band's own territory of Saddleworth Moor, with one photo including the war memorial on the hill known as Pots And Pans, above the village of Greenfield. The photographs of the band members were taken by Peter Chatterton at the University of London Observatory near Hatfield, the 'BJH' lettering (curiously, the full band name doesn't appear anywhere on the album artwork) was designed by Les, and the butterfly is based on a map of air routes!

'The Life You Lead' (Les Holroyd)

The album gets underway with a song and an arrangement which would have been quite at home on a Bee Gees album at the height of their commercial success. Les's medium-paced opener originally had the working title 'Choices', and the lyrics concern the choices we make in our relationships and everyday lives which shape our future selves. Musically it chugs along happily without ever threatening to turn into a Barclays classic.

'Lady Macbeth' (John Lees)

John's first contribution to the album, however, is most definitely a contender for classic Barclay James Harvest status, with its opening air of brooding menace and Steve Pigott's dramatic keyboard effects leading up to the explosive centre section. Stung by criticism in the recording studio that the lyrics of 'John Lennon's Guitar' were too literal and naïve, John, as he put it, 'went away and wrote a very devious one'. Fans' speculation as to the subject of 'Lady Macbeth' initially favoured Margaret Thatcher, the then Conservative Prime Minister, but more recently it has been widely assumed by fans to be a retaliatory swipe at Robert Godfrey, the orchestral arranger for Barclay James Harvest in the very early years. The reference to 'lots of young ones, singing Mahler' is, perhaps, one clue. The lyric 'Something wicked this way comes' is, of course, a quote from Shakespeare's *Macbeth* – however, it was also the title, not only of the Ray Bradbury novel which inspired John to write 'Medicine Man', but also of a 1982 album by Godfrey's band, The Enid. In March 1986 writs had been served on the four original members of Barclay James Harvest and their record companies, claiming co-authorship and royalties for ten of the band's early songs and a share of the group's earnings as the 'fifth member' of the band. The resultant court case caused not only John, Les and Mel, but also Woolly, a great deal of distress and financial hardship in fighting the case, until it was finally dismissed in the High Court in 1995, and undoubtedly contributed to the depression which eventually claimed Woolly's life. John has never confirmed or denied this interpretation of the song, although he did say that it was definitely not about Maggie Thatcher!

'Cheap The Bullet' (John Lees)

'What price your life now, how cheap the bullet', quoted above the song lyrics on the inner sleeve of the LP, was the original line that came to John, and which he jotted down as an idea for a song. The resulting denunciation of violence was the rockiest BJH song for many years and made a fine taster for the album when it was issued as a single in the UK on 5 February, with a very well produced (and expensive!) video to accompany it. Unfortunately, the German record company decided that it was too heavy for their market, whilst back home the BBC, possibly influenced by the record company's use of promotional novelty items such as 'bullet' keyrings and pens, opted not to add it to their main playlists on the grounds that it might incite violence! Nevertheless, the song proved very popular with fans and became a staple of live performances for many years. Les Holroyd offered an interesting insight into the recording process to the fan club:

> We were pretty close to distortion on a couple of tracks on the original mix; that's certainly what happened to 'Cheap The Bullet'. We had to be very, very careful bringing that up for a single because it was very close to distortion, so you have to compensate, you roll off a little bit of bass to push the vocal out.

'Welcome To The Show' (Les Holroyd)

Selected by Polydor Deutschland to be the first single from the album in Germany, Les's song contains some acid lyrical reflections on modern attitudes in general and the superficiality of the music business in particular. Les also played the Dire Straits-ish guitar at the end. The song was heavily played by German radio and the band made at least three TV appearances miming to it, not least a slot on NDR's *Musikladen* programme with a well-thought-out video collage which is almost worthy of official promo video status. Although the single didn't chart, the exposure certainly helped the album to do so.

'John Lennon's Guitar' (John Lees)

This autobiographical song was based on an incident which occurred way back in 1970, whilst BJH were recording the *Once Again* album at EMI's Abbey Road Studios. During a break in proceedings, producer Norman Smith rummaged in a cupboard and produced the very same blond Gibson Epiphone Casino which John Lennon had played during the Beatles' famous 1969 performance on the roof of the Apple building in London's Savile Row. John Lees leapt at the chance to play one of his heroes' guitars, and duly used it to record 'Galadriel'. Not everyone appreciated the somewhat naïve writing style, as John wryly recalled:

> The song was written in about two or three hours, and it was one of these that just flowed out; because of its literal use of names and things like that, I actually had to change the lyric, because people thought it sounded amateurish!

John's original demo version (released fifteen years later on the *All Is Safely Gathered In* box set) included, unsurprisingly, plenty of guitar, but on the album recording, perversely, there is virtually no guitar to be heard. That was rectified in the live arena, where the song really came into its own with a rip-roaring Lees guitar solo leading the band into what can only be described as a boogie! The studio version was released in Germany as the third single from the album, to mark the tenth anniversary of Lennon's death. A live recording of 'John Lennon's Guitar' appears on the 2016 Esoteric label deluxe two-CD set of *Caught In The Light*, forming part of a bonus disc comprising half of a 1992 concert at London's Town And Country Club.

'Halfway To Freedom' (Les Holroyd)

Les's massed acoustic guitar-led anthem to the people of the former Soviet Union and Eastern Bloc proved prophetic: between the song being written and the album being released, events had overtaken everyone and the Berlin Wall had finally fallen. In the album's sleeve notes, Les dedicated the song to the people of Germany, and in a fan club interview explained his motives for writing the song at that particular time:

> After doing the East Berlin concert [in 1987] I was convinced that the Wall was definitely going to be down before Christmas. It wasn't specifically about Germany, I must confess that. I think what sparked it off was Romania because I'd been following that for quite some time. I just couldn't believe what was happening out there.

'Halfway To Freedom', alongside 'Cheap The Bullet', 'Lady Macbeth' and 'The Life You Lead', was included on a promo-only sampler CD, but a halfway completed mix of 'Halfway' was used, with some minor differences from the finished track. The finished version became the second single from the album in Germany, and was showcased at a TV event called *Guten Abend, Deutschland* ('Good Evening, Germany'). This programme was recorded in East Berlin with popular compères from both East and West Germany, and broadcast right across the newly reunited country – the first time such an event had taken place since the division of Germany after the Second World War.

'African Nights' (Les Holroyd)

This album has a strong backwards-looking flavour, and here Les reminisces about touring South Africa in September and October 1972. The 'friend whose name was Farr' was bluesman Gary Farr, who supported BJH on that tour, travelling with them in an old VW campervan, and who released a number of solo albums between 1969 and 1984. Just over halfway through, the initially low-key arrangement bursts into life with some very lively drum sounds, and fans commented very favourably on Mel Pritchard's form. The man himself was honest enough to admit in an interview for the fan club magazine that he hadn't actually played the part in question: 'That was Steve Pigott – he had this idea of doing something with the end, so we sat down and worked this thing out.' It was typical of Mel to downplay his own role, but between the two of them they created a high point of the album.

'Psychedelic Child' (John Lees)

Introduced by an ersatz motorbike engine and a wailing siren, John's 'Psychedelic Child' harked back to the hippy era of the late sixties. The piece is one of BJH's occasional forays into straightforward driving rock, and the tongue-in-cheek lyric is a 'stream of consciousness' listing of cultural icons of the period. Some of the less obvious references include 'My Little Red Book', the first single by American band Love, The UFO Club, a well-known psychedelic venue in London, and 'Ballad Of A Thin Man', a track from Bob Dylan's 1965 LP *Highway 61 Revisited*. Blow Up, credited on the inner sleeve of the album as the inspiration for the song, were a local band, friends of John's who recorded at his studio, and Josh was their manager.

'Where Do We Go' (Les Holroyd)

Les's stately evocation of lost love proved very popular with fans, although, somewhat surprisingly, the song has not been performed live to date by any incarnation of the band. Musically, Les's admiration for the big ballads of Chicago's Peter Cetera is apparent, while the 'woman in love' references recall the brothers Gibb once more. Extra colour is added by the sax solo from Andy Hamilton, best known for his work with Dexy's Midnight Runners, Duran Duran and Wham.

'Origin Earth' (John Lees) [on CD and MC only]

This song was inspired by the sci-fi novel *Eon* by Greg Bear, a copy of which was given to John in April 1989 by one of the founders of the International Barclay James Harvest Fan Club, sci-fi buff Kevin Goodman. The tale concerns a mysterious structure which appears in orbit around the Earth and turns out to be not from some alien civilisation, but from the future of Earth itself. Continuing the precedent set with the previous Barclays album, *Face To Face*, the CD and cassette versions of *Welcome To The Show* included two songs which did not appear on the vinyl LP, and 'Origin Earth' has, to the best of our knowledge, never been released on vinyl.

'If Love Is King' (John Lees)

Another John Lees lyrical enigma for fans to unravel! A heartfelt vocal, a repetitive keyboard hookline and some outstanding guitar work turn it into a standout track and one of the strongest – and most intriguing – songs on the album. BJH aficionados had to wait sixteen years to hear it performed live when Woolly Wolstenholme sang the lead vocal at a few concerts on the 2006 John Lees' Barclay James Harvest U.K. tour. Themes of the shallowness and ultimate worthlessness of riches and instant gratification are recurring motifs in John's writing, but the man himself has never commented further on this particular lyric – until now:

> If this song were a painting, it would be an abstract. The blind man and the no count are one and the same, as are the rich man and the prisoner of the real king (money). If love is king (kings have crowns) and music is the food of love, then love's crown in this instance could be food or money. Either way, there are no winners here, only losers, as someone basically ate love – metaphorically speaking.

'Shadows On The Sky' (Les Holroyd) [on CD and MC only]

Making its first public appearance as the B-side of 'Cheap The Bullet', Les's 'Shadows On The Sky' was an impressive advertisement for the album, featuring some thought-provoking lyrics about big game such as elephants and rhinos being hunted to extinction. On the African plains, it's possible to see for great distances, and animals look like shadows on the horizon, hence the lyrical reference to shadows on the sky. The unusual 'backwards' guitar solo was played by guest musician Mike Hehir, then of Sad Café. The single version of 'Shadows On The Sky' was actually an edit of an early take, and quite different from the one which eventually appeared on the album, as Les explained:

> That was an edited version. It was all right, but it wasn't musically correct; there was half a chorus missing on the second chorus where it went into the middle eight, there were odd vocals missing. I think on the original mix we put the oral exciter on it and tended to overdo it a little bit.

For live shows the song was developed into a big audience participation finale, closing the show in fine style, and was included in Barclay James Harvest Featuring Les Holroyd live sets up until 2007.

Related Song:

'Stand Up' (R. Bolland/F. Bolland)

This 1992 single is a real curio in the Barclay James Harvest canon. It's unique amongst BJH singles in that it wasn't written by the band – the song comes from a concept album called *Darwin – The Evolution*, which was written by Dutch brothers Rob and Ferdi Bolland and issued under the name The Bolland Project. BJH's contribution came about through their manager, David Walker, who also looked after Status Quo. Quo had scored a big hit with The Bolland Brothers' song 'In The Army Now', and when the brothers were looking for guest musicians for their album, Walker thought that this song about the destruction of the environment would be just right for the Barclays. It appeared in four different single formats in the UK, including a limited edition CD single in a large butterfly-shaped pack, all credited to Barclay James Harvest. The German single, by contrast, is credited to The Bolland Project. The extended version from one of the CD singles appears on the 2016 two-disc remaster of *Welcome To The Show*, whilst a live rendition is included on the same year's *Caught In The Light* set.

Caught In The Light (1993)

Personnel:
John Lees: electric and acoustic guitars, keyboards and vocals
Les Holroyd: bass, electric and classical guitars, keyboards and vocals
Mel Pritchard: drums and percussion
Kevin McAlea: keyboards
Darrin Tidsey: assistance with programming
Recorded at Friarmere Studios, Delph, December 1992 to April 1993
Mastered at The Town House, London
Producer: Barclay James Harvest and Martin Lawrence
Engineer: Martin Lawrence
Record Label: Polydor
UK release date: 14 June 1993
Highest chart places: Germany: 82, Switzerland: 33

The nineties had begun auspiciously for Barclay James Harvest, with two German gold albums in the shape of the 1990 studio set, *Welcome To The Show*, and a TV-advertised *Best Of* on the Polystar label which made the top ten in November 1991, and now they needed to capitalise on the renewed interest. An extensive U.K. and Continental tour celebrating the 25th anniversary of the band's formation kept them busy in the early months of 1992. On their return, the band members set to work writing and demoing material for a new studio album, with old friend Martin Lawrence drafted back in as co-producer. Shortly before recording began, John completely rebuilt and re-equipped his own facility, Friarmere, moving the studio into the basement and converting the rest of the building into flats.

The new studio set up was digital, based around three Alesis ADATs and an Akai hard disc recorder. This permitted instrumental parts to be recorded individually and then synchronised with a computerised time track. The disadvantage of this way of recording was that the members of the band didn't need to be in the studio at the same time, but instead worked on their own songs with co-producer Martin Lawrence, and there was practically no live playing on the recording. On the plus side, costs were kept to a minimum, whilst still yielding recordings of a high technical standard. The album was completed in April 1993, and after some debate over a suitable title, with *Silver Wings* and *Feel The Silence* under consideration, the decision was made to go with *Caught In The Light*, taken from a prologue written by Les Holroyd, and originally intended to introduce the opening track of the album. The album was released by Polydor in June with little fanfare. Plans to release a vinyl LP were dropped, advertising was minimal, and even the band themselves didn't seem to be eager to push it: in the live set at nine open-air concerts in Germany which were ostensibly arranged to promote the new album, only two songs from it were performed. John Lees revealed to the band's fan club, just months after *Caught In The Light*'s release, that he had been disappointed with the album:

> When we started recording, I'd visions of us getting back to the old days when we worked together as a group on arrangements and put our own style and instrumentation on each other's songs and, most important to my mind, the rich vocal harmonies which were such a distinctive feature of our early records. These qualities I've always personally thought were the common thread that made my own songs, those of Les and, in times past Woolly's songs, so complementary to each other. What made us a band, what gave us the BJH sound. Unfortunately, it was not to be, and the amount of creative input on each other's songs continues to decrease on each new album.

Caught In The Light came out at a difficult time for the band, overshadowed by personal tragedy (John's father passed away in 1992) and the looming threat of Robert Godfrey's impending court action against them, and the overall mood is one of sadness and regret. The paucity of up-tempo numbers on what is a very long album adds to that impression, and reviewers were not impressed. With minimal record company backing, too, sales were dismal, clocking up only forty-odd thousand Europe-wide, compared with over two hundred and fifty thousand for *Welcome To The Show* a mere three years earlier. More than a quarter of a century on, *Caught In The Light* is not generally regarded as one of their best offerings. It's not a bad album but is rather long and slow, and in some ways resembles two solo albums welded together. Whilst it is not, it must be said, up to the standard of some of their earlier work, it still has its adherents amongst the band's fans, and contains some strong songs.

Sleeve Design

The album cover was not the one originally planned. John had come up with the idea of combining the best elements of Monet's 'Water Lilies' and The Beatles' *Revolver* cover, but at least one of the band members was unhappy the resulting design, and it was unceremoniously consigned to the bin. Instead Les suggested commissioning Rodney Matthews, who had previously designed many album covers, including Asia's *Aqua*. Les was a fan of his work, owning a calendar featuring his paintings, and the new painting was based on Les's concept of butterfly-shaped spaceships. In his book *Countdown To Millennium*, Matthews gave an insight into the process, and revealed an earlier connection with the band:

> I was pleased to be invited to participate in the cover design for this album because I can remember my band Squidd supporting Barclay James Harvest at a Bath University gig in the early 1970s! The design concept of this image belongs to Les Holroyd, who explained how all their album covers have a butterfly included somewhere. As I was producing the first two rough sketches, my wife Karin, who also trained as an illustrator, happened to be in my studio and remarked that she considered a lighter, rounder butterfly would be more appropriate for this style of music. Karin did a sketch to illustrate her meaning and, with a few amendments, it was chosen by the band.

'Who Do We Think We Are' (Les Holroyd)

In the run-up to the release of *Caught In The Light* there was some debate about the running time of the album, and a number of cuts were made to reduce the running time to a still somewhat unwieldy seventy minutes. One of the songs to be shortened was the opening track, Les Holroyd's 'Who Do We Think We Are?', written on the subject of mankind's destruction of the Earth. The opening verse, which was intended to form a prelude to the main song, was omitted from the recording, although, oddly, the words were still included in the printed lyrics in the CD booklet, and the album title itself is taken from the missing verse:

> All around we're caught in the light of a thousand suns
> Riding the wind of eternal years
> Watching the Earth die before our eyes
> Hearing the world crying in our ears

The song was issued in edited form as the lead track on a German promo-only CD, in an attempt to gain some airplay, but no commercially available single was ever released from the album. Barclay James Harvest themselves never performed the song on stage, but in 2011 it made its live debut as the opening song at Barclay James Harvest Featuring Les Holroyd concerts, a position it has held ever since. The live version, complete with the 'lost' verse sung by Les with a vocoder effect, following a pre-recorded stage introduction, can be heard on that band's 2016 double live CD, *Retrospective*.

'Knoydart' (John Lees)

'Knoydart' was inspired by one of John Lees' favourite places, a peninsula on the west coast of the Scottish Highlands, and includes many references to local landmarks. The first line of the lyrics should read 'heading for Mallaig', not 'racing for Mallaig', the town from which the ferry crosses the Sound Of Sleat (the correct spelling) to Knoydart. Spanish John, Ladhar Bheinn, Kinloch Hourn and Inverie are all places on the peninsula. There is an affectionate nod to John's friends with whom he visited Knoydart in the dedication to the 'ugly bastards' contained within the album credits. The song lyrics certainly succeed in conjuring up the wild and beautiful landscape, although the decidedly inorganic arrangement, with chiefly computerised instrumentation, rather undermines the effect.

'Copii Romania' (Les Holroyd)

Les cited 'Copii Romania' as the favourite of his songs from *Caught In The Light*. The subject matter is the turmoil in Romania following the collapse of the Communist regime and the execution of its leader, Nicolae Ceauşescu, in the Romanian Revolution of December 1989. The English subtitle, 'Children Of Romania', reflected Les's concerns, and he announced that all of his royalties from the song would be donated to the fund for the orphan children of Romania. It's a slow ballad with the lyrics incorporating some local colour with references to *lăutari* (members of a professional clan of Romani musicians, the name being derived from *lăută*, the Romanian word for lute), and 'the mighty Karpatii', the Carpathian mountains.

'Back To Earth' (John Lees)

'Back To Earth' is another very personal song, this time from the pen of John Lees, written following the death of his father in 1992. The lyrics speak of John's loss and his regret that he couldn't be there in his father's final days. It's a very moving tribute, but again the lack of a band performance shows with some unsympathetic synthesised bass and MIDI drum sounds. John dedicated the song not only to the loving memory of his father but also to all those who mourn for the loss of someone they love. In the late 1990s, John would donate a gold-plated Morse key to the Oldham Amateur Radio Club, of which both he and his father were members: the Fred Lees Memorial Trophy was presented annually to a club member who had given exceptional service during the year. Fred had been a member of the club since the 1930s and had undertaken listening duties during the Second World War, intercepting messages which were then submitted to Bletchley Park for decoding.

'Cold War' (Les Holroyd)

Les dedicated this anti-war lament to his cousin Marguerette, who was living in the former Yugoslavia at a time when the country was racked by a bitter civil war. The lyrics capture the vicious circle of the country's history, in which the contemporary call to arms echoes the songs of the partisans of old, and 'the fears of the past bring tears of today'. The classical guitar at the end of the song was played by Les, who told us that it was his first instrument as a youngster, before he took up piano and later bass.

'Forever Yesterday' (John Lees)

John's historical song concerns the shameful history of the Highland clearances. In the 19th century the Scottish highlanders were mostly tenant farmers, using the traditional runrig system, whereby each farmer had several non-contiguous strips of land. Their English absentee landlords were content as long as the land was unsuitable for more profitable use. However, new breeds of sheep such as the black-faced Lintons and Great Cheviots were capable of surviving on the bleak highland hillsides, and the landowners saw the chance of huge profits. The farmers were unceremoniously evicted, often by force, and a large number went to the New World. John Morrison (Murdo) and Neil Morrison, who are credited with the inspiration for the song, used to live on Knoydart, and it was whilst John Lees was there on holiday that the history of the clearances first came to his attention. The original recording of 'Forever Yesterday' included a coda featuring a particularly fine guitar solo, which was unforgivably excised from the CD (although, unaccountably, left on the cassette issue) to shorten the running time of the album. A 2016 remaster of the album saw the song restored to its full glory. Even in its butchered form, it's an affecting piece, and in full it's magnificent.

'The Great Unknown' (Les Holroyd)
An understated, churchy-sounding keyboard sets the scene for this reflective, romantic song about love and growing older before the guitar and electronic drums come crashing in for the second half. The piece benefits from one of the better, more fully realised arrangements on the album. Some well-thought-out vocal variations and more vocoder effects embellish the main melody before the final fade-out.

'Spud-U-Like' (John Lees)
John's next offering was given the subtitle 'David's Rock Song', the man in question being David Walker of Handle Artists, BJH's then management company, who was particularly keen on the inclusion of something more up-tempo on the album. The song was already some years old, but producer Martin Lawrence persuaded John to finish it and record it for this album. Its new title was inspired, if that's the right word, by a video game called *Spud's Adventure*, released in 1991 on the Game Boy platform, as well as cheekily appropriating the name of a chain of fast-food restaurants. The song unfavourably compares video games and the culture of instant gratification with the more lasting pleasures of rock and roll. It must be said, though, that the song divided listeners into those who enjoyed its undemanding, tongue-in-cheek rock and those who found it crass and superficial, and the sound effects merely annoying.

'Silver Wings' (Les Holroyd)
Les described *Caught In The Light* as 'a very personal album', and that's certainly true of this ballad, which captures the anguish caused by the end of a relationship in a beautiful and bittersweet fashion. The Peter Cetera influence is there again, but Les manages to stay just the right side of maudlin or cloying, and there's enough musical variation in the arrangement to keep the listener's interest. This is the only piece on the album to clock in at less than four minutes, and is all the better for it.

'Once More' (John Lees)
It might seem a little odd for a musician to quote himself and re-write from scratch one of his best-loved anthems, but it makes perfect sense as John's way of proving the original's pedigree at a time when doubts had been cast on the authorship of 'Mocking Bird'. In 'Once More', the title harking back to the *Once Again* album on which 'Mocking Bird' first appeared, John also quotes musically from 'Galadriel' and mentions 'Pools Of Blue', which was written at the same time. The end result is a piece which, whilst strongly reminiscent of its illustrious predecessor, is also a completely new minor BJH classic in its own right, lending weight to John's assertion that 'they'll never kill the mockingbird'.

'A Matter Of Time' (Les Holroyd)
Les returns to the subject of relationship issues in the reflective 'A Matter Of Time'. This was one of only two songs from the new album (along with John's

'Back To Earth') to be included in the setlist at a series of live dates in Germany at the time of the album's release. It's possible that the band intended to perform more of the album on a longer tour planned for that autumn, but poor ticket sales and an unenthusiastic response to the album meant that the tour never went ahead. Les later performed this song again with his own band, Barclay James Harvest Featuring Les Holroyd, in live shows in 2004 and 2012.

'Ballad Of Denshaw Mill' (John Lees)

This slow-burner with folky undertones had an interesting genesis, inspired by the presence on John's property of fragments of an old water wheel – this turned out to be a remnant of Denshaw Mill, an old woollen 'fulling mill' which operated until the late 1880s, and was already derelict by the time of the first war, when the fictional legend in the song takes place. The piece was first presented for possible inclusion on the *Ring Of Changes* album but was not adopted at the time. The intro and coda of the finished version were actually taken directly from John's original demo, with John's lead guitar overdubbed, and most of the recording was programmed by him, with additional keyboard parts from Kevin McAlea and percussion from Mel Pritchard. Thomas Wrigley (father of local poet Ammon), who worked at the mill in its day, pronounced it 'as rotten a place as ever fouled the green earth of Saddleworth'. One of the reasons it was so foul was that part of the 'fulling' process involved cleaning the raw sheep's wool to rid it of dirt and oils before it was spun. What's so foul about that? Well, the cleaning agent used at the time was stale urine ... The 'legend' was purely John's invention, but the site itself is an evocative part of the history of this area and a relic of the industrial revolution. The area is part of the Friarmere division of Saddleworth, known locally as the Darkside. Harold McKlintock, to whose memory the song is dedicated, was an old friend and neighbour, and a source of inspiration to John when he wrote the song.

River Of Dreams (1997)

Personnel:
John Lees: lead, acoustic and electric guitars, keyboards and vocals
Les Holroyd: bass, acoustic, electric, 12-string electric and classical guitars, keyboards and vocals
Mel Pritchard: drums and percussion
Kevin McAlea: keyboards
Colin Browne: guitars and keyboards
Jeff Leach: keyboards, string arrangement on 'Back In The Game'
Recorded at Friarmere Studios, Delph, February 1996 to February 1997
Producer: Barclay James Harvest and Martin Lawrence
Engineer: Martin Lawrence
Record Label: Polydor GmbH
European release date: 26 May 1997 (not released in the UK)
Highest chart places: Germany: 71, Switzerland: 33

On 21 March 1995, the long-running legal action by Robert Godfrey against the members of Barclay James Harvest and their record companies was finally brought to an end in the High Court, with the judge dismissing both of Godfrey's actions, following which band and management met up in July to discuss the future of Barclay James Harvest. Given the disappointing reaction to *Caught In The Light* and the cancellation of a planned German tour in autumn 1993 because of poor ticket sales, John, at least, was by no means certain that the band should carry on at all. However, the success of 1991's *The Best Of Barclay James* Harvest album in Germany led Polydor to consider a second volume, and it was suggested that the band could record a couple of brand new songs at Friarmere, which would then be included on the compilation as an incentive for die-hard fans. When this proposed compilation was first delayed, then ditched altogether, the band had more time to work on new material and decided to carry on with a view to recording an entire album. In September, they met again and two new songs were chosen to be recorded, Les's 'Yesterday's Heroes' and John's 'River Of Dreams'. The band were then offered the opportunity to appear at a prestigious Pop and Rock Festival in the Swiss Alps at Visp, giving them the perfect platform to prove that BJH were back in business and to premiere the new songs live at that event and at three low-key German warm-up dates.

February 1996 saw John, Les and Mel back in John's Friarmere Studios recording the new album, but there was a question mark over who would release it. Polydor U.K.'s interest in the band had been on the wane for some time, so it came as no great surprise to anyone when they declined to take up an option on a further two studio albums, putting an end to BJH's twenty-year relationship with the label. However, the German arm of the company was keen to sign the band, and in May it was announced that a new contract had been agreed with Polydor GmbH. In June 1996 the fan club did an on the spot report at Friarmere for the club magazine, and found the band in good humour, with Les enthusing about his new Rickenbacker guitar, and John even describing how he and Les had ended up playing acoustic guitars together on one session, something which hadn't happened for many years. July saw the band taking a break for family holidays, and there was another hiatus when co-producer Martin Lawrence was absent because of a prior engagement touring with Joe Longthorne. Whether the delays affected morale within the band, or whether the initial enthusiasm simply wore off, the reports coming out of the studio became less enthusiastic, with John being particularly unhappy with the state of affairs. He felt that the spirit of co-operation which had marked the recording of 'River Of Dreams' and 'Yesterday's Heroes' had evaporated, with Les and himself working separately on their own songs – the very thing which had upset him so much about *Caught In The Light* and which he had been promised would not happen this time. John expressed his frustration in a 1998 interview:

> As soon as we got the deal with Polydor and we came into the studio it went right back to square one, people working on their own. All those songs were wasted because they never turned out like they were supposed to turn out.

Les had a somewhat different view of what went wrong:

> I still think it sounds quite fresh compared with the last few albums, but I think we could have taken it a stage further, and personally I think we should have done it in a different studio. I think we should have got away from the area and totally isolated ourselves from all the normal domestic things that go on around you.

Mel, though, was happy with the recording:

> I think it's as good as anything we've done, in fact in some ways I think it's a lot better than some of the things we've done in the past. I've got to say that it took a little bit longer than was expected, but it was just one of those things. John had booked his holiday and stuff like that. In terms of the overall sounds and the songs, yeah, I was happy.

Recording dragged on into 1997, and by the time that the album was finally completed, a year had elapsed since they first began work at Friarmere. Released on 26 May in Germany and Switzerland, *River Of Dreams* managed a small improvement on its predecessor's chart showing, reaching number 71, but it quickly slipped out of the rankings, and it became clear that this was to be no major comeback for the band. In spite of the difficulties and the muted response, the album is really rather good. There was enough of the band spirit about the recordings to convince most fans that it was a genuine BJH album and a significant improvement over *Caught In The Light* – at least those fans who were actually aware of its existence. To the consternation of the band's loyal domestic audience, Polydor U.K. chose not to release the album at all, and fans who wanted to hear the new album were forced to buy expensive imported copies. To this date, the album has never received an official release in the band's home country and has long been unavailable in the shops elsewhere.

Sleeve Design

The CD cover artwork was created for the Hamburg Art & Werbeteam agency by German graphic designer Dirk Rudolph, who is best known for his work with German acts such as Rammstein, Phillip Boa, Scorpions and Die Toten Hosen. He was also responsible for the cover of the previous year's worldwide hit album, *18 Til I Die*, by Bryan Adams. The design for *River Of Dreams* was based on a stock photo of a droplet of water suspended above concentric ripples in water, with the only change for the final version being the addition of a 'water droplet' butterfly and the band name and album title lettering above. The small and rather gloomy-looking photo of the band in a local church towards the back of the CD booklet was taken by Les's brother-in-law, Chris Roberts.

'Back In The Game' (Les Holroyd)

Guest keyboard player, arranger and composer Jeff Leach wrote the string overture which gets the album underway in an echo of former BJH glories. An acoustic guitar intro takes over, before John steps in with some fine lead guitar reminiscent of the band's mid-seventies sound, matching the song's backward-looking lyrics. John contributes backing vocals on the choruses, and there are echoes of 1970s songs by other artists, with a Toto-esque piano riff and a part of the chorus which bears a distinct resemblance, lyrically and melodically, to a line in The Kinks' 1978 song, 'A Rock 'n' Roll Fantasy'. 'Back In The Game', minus the string overture, was issued as a one-track, promo-only CD single in Germany.

'River Of Dreams' (John Lees)

The first and only time that John Lees wrote the title track of a Barclay James Harvest album, and it's a good one! It begins with a country-ish introduction, before gradually developing into a catchy sing-along – in stark contrast to the lyrics, which deal with looking back on life in disillusionment. This was one of the first two songs to be recorded, at a time when the band were still collaborating in the studio, and made its live debut in November 1995. John's jaundiced view of his latter-day life and musical career is clearly influenced by the recent court case and the decline in the band's fortunes. When John later got back together with Woolly Wolstenholme and their new band went on tour, the song was performed live with a completely new arrangement. Turning it into a slower, piano-led torch song was an inspired decision, more in keeping with the song's sentiments. In that guise, it is most affecting, and very well received by live audiences. That version, with Jeff Leach on piano, can be heard on the album, *Revival – Live 1999*, released under the band name Barclay James Harvest Through The Eyes Of John Lees, whilst later readings with Jez Smith performing a breathtaking, bluesy piano backing appear on *The Bloomsbury Theatre, London, 30th October 2009* and *The 50th Anniversary Concert* live sets.

'Yesterday's Heroes' (Les Holroyd/Kevin McAlea)
The other song to be recorded at the start of the album sessions was Les's 'Yesterday's Heroes', his strongest song for many years. It's a long, moody and powerful piece, and, in common with the songs which come before it on the album, has a very retrospective theme. The lyrics are aimed squarely at those who consider the band to be a spent force, 'those who try to keep the flame from burning' and dismiss them as 'yesterday's heroes'. Recent events had prompted both of the main songwriters in the band to do some soul-searching and looking back, with strikingly different results. The arrangement of the song wasn't finished when it came to recording at Friarmere, so guest keyboard player Kevin McAlea was drafted in to complete it. 'Yesterday's Heroes' was also performed live by Barclay James Harvest Featuring Les Holroyd on their orchestral tour in 2006, and a recording of that rendition appears on the *Classic Meets Rock* live double CD.

'Children Of The Disappeared' (John Lees)
John's next offering is a departure from his usual style, and is a brilliant evocation of the climate of fear affecting the parents of young children in these less innocent times than those of his youth. Musically, the sparse, piano-led beginning and end, and the beautiful pizzicato string accompaniment recall the melodies of Love's *Forever Changes*, whilst the middle section takes BJH into previously unexplored areas with hints of world music and chant – still innovative after all those years! – before returning to the classic Barclay James Harvest lead guitar sound. A magnificent and poignant piece. Sadly, it has never been performed live by any incarnation of the band.

'Pool Of Tears' (John Lees)
A total contrast here, as John shows his lighter side with a song about lost love. There is a touch of 'Origin Earth' about the melody, but the arrangement has an unusual feel, courtesy of 'jazzy' Jeff Leach on the keys. Some early copies of the CDs mistakenly rendered the song title as 'Pools Of Tears' in the booklet and on the back inlay, but this was corrected to the one which John actually sings on later pressings.

'Do You Believe In Dreams (Same Chance For Everyone)' (Les Holroyd)
Back to Les for another song with lyrical roots in the group's past, recalling the times when they 'sang where kings and presidents could change the world, just standing at the wall'. It seems clear that Les is bewildered by John's disillusionment and his wish to return to an earlier sound and ethos of Barclay James Harvest – 'the years of sacrifice', as Les's lyric puts it. A comparison of

Les and John's songs on *River Of Dreams* makes it pretty clear that the two mainstays of the band in compositional terms couldn't be further apart in their vision of the group's future, so it should really be no surprise that this album would be Barclay James Harvest's swansong.

'(Took Me) So Long' (Les Holroyd)

This is a slower, more introspective piece from Les, showcasing some more of his classical guitar expertise as well as some moody lead playing from John. A contrasting middle eight and some inventive key changes add interest and prevent the song from becoming just another romantic ballad.

'Mr. E' (John Lees)

John's affection for The Beatles is in evidence again here with a musical quote from 'Strawberry Fields Forever', but the lyrics here are as devious as anything he's written. Clearly, one interpretation would be that he's referring to the drug ecstasy, but the song can also be read on lots of other levels. John performed the song in concert on the band's 1997 German tour as a solo acoustic piece, with the other musicians leaving the stage. He introduced it enigmatically, saying that E stood for ecstasy, envy and emulation, but that the song had many meanings, and anybody who guessed all of them would be doing very well! Ultimately, the subject, as John undoubtedly intended, was a mystery, but he offers a tantalising clue now, inviting us to think of the lyric as a conversation. Thus it can be read as a dialogue, personifying the internal battle of motivations and impulses, good and bad, which drive us all; recreational drugs representing just one of the siren voices whispering in our ears ...

'Three Weeks To Despair' (John Lees)

No doubts here, as John tackles the subject of homelessness. Inspired by two articles in *The Sunday Times* written by Margarette Driscoll, the song has a dreamy melody, almost like a lullaby. The chilling recorded quotes scattered through the piece are from a homeless man who John and Martin Lawrence met on the streets in Stockport, and a salutary reminder that, as John put it in a postscript to the lyrics in the CD booklet, 'Behind every tatty sleeping bag and cardboard box there is a human being with a family, a history and a personality.'

'The Time Of Our Lives' (Les Holroyd)

A reflective opening gives way to acoustic guitars and an anthemic chorus, to end the album on a more upbeat note. Fittingly, perhaps, the very last track on the very last album by the original Barclay James Harvest is a comment on modern mores and the state of the world, not too far removed from the subjects which had occupied the songwriters' thoughts thirty years earlier.

Live Albums

Barclay James Harvest Live (1974)

'Summer Soldier'; 'Medicine Man'; 'Crazy City'; 'After The Day'; 'The Great 1974 Mining Disaster'; 'Galadriel'; 'Negative Earth'; 'She Said'; 'Paper Wings'; 'For No One'; 'Mockingbird'.

Recorded at: London Theatre Royal, Drury Lane, 30 June 1974; Liverpool Stadium, 31 August 1974
Producer: Rodger Bain
Engineer: Brian Humphries
Mixed at Island Studios, London
Sleeve Design: Vincent McEvoy and Keith Davis; photography by Alex Agor and Tim Brown
Released: November 1974, Polydor
Chart Position: UK: 40

Barclay James Harvest's reputation rested as much on the quality of their live performances as on their studio output, so it was logical that their new record label would wish to showcase their live prowess, whilst also obtaining the right to issue some of the classic songs originally recorded for EMI's Harvest label. The tour to promote *Everyone Is Everybody Else* culminated in two shows at Liverpool Stadium on 29 June and London's Theatre Royal in Drury Lane on 30 June, and it was planned to film and record those two concerts for promotional use and for the band's first live album, with the Island Mobile Studio. However, in Liverpool, the band's road crew discovered a dangerous electrical problem when setting up, and the gig had to be postponed to August. The London show didn't go smoothly, either, with Woolly's Mellotron 300 drifting in and out of tune alarmingly all night. The record company didn't want to delay the release of the live album more than necessary, so opted to mix the offending Mellotron down as far as possible, then to overdub the minimum of new parts to cover it up for the double live album and use recordings from the rescheduled Liverpool gig where necessary. From listening to an original recording of the London show, it's possible to say with a degree of certainty that the majority of songs are from the London show, with the Liverpool recordings being 'Negative Earth', 'She Said' and, possibly, 'Paper Wings'.

Barclay James Harvest Live actually sounds remarkably good, considering its inauspicious beginnings, capturing the live energy and magic of a fine band at their peak. Many of the performances add a great deal of power and impact to their (already impressive) studio counterparts, and 'For No One', in particular, benefits from a superb, chiming finale in place of the slightly anti-climactic fade of the original. The original double LP suffered slightly from a certain muddiness to the sound, but the 2005 remastered CD issued by Eclectic Discs brought new clarity to what was already a classic live album. The band's growing popularity (and the very reasonable 1974 selling price of

£2.94) meant that the album edged its way into the charts at number 40 – at last, after six years of hard work, their first-ever chart record!

Live Tapes (1978)

'Child Of The Universe'; 'Rock 'N' Roll Star'; 'Poor Man's Moody Blues'; 'Mockingbird'; 'Hard Hearted Woman'; 'One Night'; 'Taking Me Higher'; 'Suicide?'; 'Crazy City'; 'Jonathan'; 'For No One'; 'Polk Street Rag'; 'Hymn'.

Recorded at: Liverpool Empire, Hammersmith Odeon and Croydon Fairfield Halls in October 1976, and various concerts in October/November 1977
Producer: Barclay James Harvest, assisted by David Rohl
Engineer: David Rohl, Steve C. Smith, assisted by Ian Southerington
Mixed at Strawberry Studios North; mastered at Utopia Studios, London
Sleeve Design: Concept by Barclay James Harvest, design by Jo Mirowski. Photos by Christopher B. Roberts and Martyn Goddard
Released: 9 June 1978, Polydor
Chart Position: Germany: 33

A number of concerts on Barclay James Harvest's 1976 autumn tour of the UK were recorded with a view to producing a live album for the American market only, and at the beginning of March 1977, Polydor UK issued a live EP in a picture sleeve, comprising 'Rock 'N' Roll Star' and 'Medicine Man' from these recordings. By October 1977 it had been decided to release the album in Europe as well, but the plan had to be changed again when the proposed deal to release the album in America fell through. Since Europe would now be the only market for the LP, and the 1974 live album was still available there, it was decided to avoid too much duplication of tracks by using more recent material recorded for a documentary film in Germany on the 1977 tour, and to make it another double album rather than the originally envisaged single LP. 'The World Goes On' and 'Hymn For The Children' were dropped from the tracklisting, and four *Gone To Earth* songs, namely 'Poor Man's Moody Blues', 'Hard Hearted Woman', 'Taking Me Higher' and 'Hymn', added. It's not known exactly where each song was recorded, but the 1976 songs were taped at the Liverpool Empire (14 October), Hammersmith Odeon (19) and Croydon Fairfield Halls (24), whilst some of the 1977 tracks were recorded in the UK and some in Hamburg. The LP was delayed when the band was unhappy with the quality of printing on the sleeve, which was largely designed by themselves, and by a last-minute change of album title: it was to be called, like the documentary film, *Caught Live*, until a fan pointed out that the Moody Blues had recently released a double live album with the title *Caught Live – Plus Five*. For BJH to release a very similarly titled album including the song 'Poor Man's Moody Blues' would have given the critics a field day, so the band acted quickly to rename the album *Live Tapes*, although the film, in a more advanced state of production, retained the original title. The album still hangs together well as a record of a band close to their artistic and commercial peak, even though the recordings are taken from two different tours. However, coming so soon after the first live album and the EP, the response in the UK was muted, despite extensive advertising. In Germany, however, where the first live album had not yet been released, the sales were much healthier, with the LP reaching number 33 in the official album chart and eventually qualifying for gold disc status with over 250,000 sales. In 2006 Eclectic Discs released a remastered double CD of *Live Tapes*, which includes the abandoned recordings from the first planned tracklisting, 'The World Goes On' and 'Hymn For The Children', plus 'Medicine Man' (not the version issued on the Live EP, which had already been included as a bonus track on a CD remaster of *Gone To Earth*, but a previously unreleased recording from the Liverpool Empire show on 14 October 1976).

A Concert For The People (Berlin) (1982)

'Berlin'; 'Loving Is Easy'; 'Mockingbird'; 'Sip Of Wine'; 'Nova Lepidoptera'; 'In Memory Of The Martyrs'; 'Life Is For Living'; 'Child Of The Universe'; 'Hymn'.

Tracklisting for limited edition German vinyl album and 2006/2010 remastered CDs: 'Love On The Line'; 'Mockingbird'; 'Rock 'N' Roll Lady'; 'Nova Lepidoptera'; 'Sip Of Wine'; 'In Memory Of The Martyrs'; 'Life Is For Living'; 'Child Of The Universe'; 'Berlin'; 'Loving Is Easy'; 'Hymn'.

Recorded at: Berlin Reichstag, 30 August 1980 by Mobile One
Producer: Barclay James Harvest, Martin Lawrence and Ian Southerington
Live Engineer: Andy Rose
Additional Recording and Mixing at Strawberry Studios, Stockport
Sleeve Design: Based on a photo of the huge crowd in front of the Reichstag on the afternoon of the show, and designed by Müller & Von Frankenburg, Hamburg
Released: January 1982 (Polystar Germany), July 1982 (Polydor UK)
Chart Positions: Germany: 1, UK: 15

On 30 August 1980, Barclay James Harvest played a concert which would become legendary in their long and illustrious history, to what proved to be their largest audience ever. The Berlin Senate's Cultural Committee had been looking to organise some major summer events, whilst Barclay James Harvest's management had been unable to find a suitable and available venue in Berlin for the band to play on their sell-out German tour in early 1980, so it was a match made in heaven. The venue selected by the Senate was to be the very steps of the Reichstag, the famous old parliament building, just yards from the Berlin Wall which had divided the city ever since the beginning of the cold war. The attendance on the day surpassed all expectations: the official police figure for the attendance was one hundred and seventy-five thousand, and unofficial estimates have put the actual numbers at anything up to a quarter of a million people, plus thousands more listening on the other side of the wall in East Berlin. The band was reaching the peak of its popularity in Germany, and this was THE gig to be seen at.

John, Les and Mel were joined on the day by Kevin McAlea on keyboards, backing vocals and saxophone, and Colin Browne on keyboards, guitar, bass and backing vocals. Two brand new songs, specially written for the occasion, were premiered: 'In Memory Of The Martyrs', a tribute to all those who had lost their lives attempting to get over the infamous Wall and flee to the West, and the upliftingly poppy 'Life Is For Living'. The band played to a very enthusiastic audience for over two and a quarter hours before they finally left the stage, and even then the announcer had to explain that the band were totally exhausted before the crowds began to disperse. Whilst the concert itself was a triumph, sadly the recording of it was not. This was in part due to some problems with John's main guitar, which had been knocked over at some point in the afternoon, but was chiefly down to some bad electrical hum which rendered large portions of the multi-track tapes unusable. Reluctant to give up on a permanent record of such an important event in the band's career (not to mention the substantial amount of money invested in the original concert), the record company, management and band decided to use as much as they could of the raw live tapes and to re-record the remainder in the Strawberry North studio to make up a single LP. This was achieved during the second half of 1981, which accounts for the long gap between the concert and the appearance of the album. In January 1982 Polystar, the TV-advertising arm of Polydor GmbH, released a limited edition 11-track album, *Berlin – A Concert For The People*, featuring two songs, 'Love On The Line' and 'Rock 'N' Roll Lady', which would not be on the standard LP once the limited version sold out. 'Limited' is a relative term in this context, as a quarter of a million copies of the Polystar version were pressed – coincidentally, exactly the number of sales required for the award of a gold disc in Germany! A combination of this marketing ploy and the intense interest and publicity which the original concert had generated helped *Berlin* straight to the top of the German album chart, achieving that coveted gold disc status. Once the limited eleven-track version was sold out in Germany, it was substituted by a nine-track edition with a different running order on the Polydor label. Fans in Britain had to wait until July for the album, when the nine-track version of the LP was finally released, in order to coincide with cinema and BBC television screenings of the film of the concert. Curiously, for the UK release the title was subtly altered to *A Concert For The People – Berlin*. Boosted by a BBC TV broadcast of the concert, the album became BJH's highest ever chart entry in Britain, entering the album chart at number 15.

Glasnost (1988)

'Poor Man's Moody Blues'; 'Alone In The Night'; 'Hold On'; 'African'; 'On The Wings Of Love'; 'Love On The Line'; 'Berlin'; 'Medicine Man'; 'Kiev'; 'Hymn'; 'Turn the Key' (on CD and MC only); 'He Said Love' (on CD and MC only).

Tracklisting for 2013 remastered and expanded 2CD set:
'Nova Lepidoptera'; 'Hold On'; 'African'; 'Love On The Line'; 'Alone In The Night';

'On The Wings Of Love'; 'Mockingbird'; 'Rock And Roll Lady'; 'He Said Love'; 'Turn the Key'; 'Medicine Man'; 'Kiev'; 'Child Of The Universe'; 'Life Is For Living'; 'Poor Man's Moody Blues'; 'Berlin'; 'Loving Is Easy'; 'Hymn'

Recorded at: Treptower Park, East Berlin, 14 July 1987, by Derks Mobile
Producer: Gregg Jackman, Barclay James Harvest and Ian Southerington
Engineer: Gregg Jackman, assisted by Karen Down
Live Engineers: Gregg Jackman, Gerd Rautenbach and Peter Brandt, assisted by Wally Nitzer
Remix Engineers: Gregg Jackman and Ian Southerington
Mixed at Advision Studios, London
Sleeve Design: No artwork credits are given for the album design, which is made up from sliced up parts of a photo of the band and audience on the day, possibly a still from the film of the concert.
Released: 5 April 1988, Polydor
Chart Position: Germany: 47, Switzerland: 30

The year 1987 marked the 750th anniversary of the founding of the city of Berlin, a jubilee marked in both East and West Germany by numerous cultural events. In East Berlin, the Communist authorities wanted to attract foreign stars and visitors, and Barclay James Harvest, famous for their 1980 concert on the western side of the Berlin Wall, were invited to repeat that feat and become the first western rock band to be permitted to play an open-air concert in the East. Initially, the plan was to hold an open-air concert on the small 'Insel der Jugend' ('Island of Youth') in the River Spree. The island could accommodate around ten thousand concertgoers, but within two weeks of the announcement of the show, the organisers were besieged with more than fifty thousand applications for tickets, and the concert was relocated to nearby Treptower Park. In the event, it was clear that the band's hitherto untested pulling power behind the Iron Curtain had been seriously underestimated, as the actual attendance on the day was variously estimated at anywhere between a hundred and thirty thousand and a hundred and seventy thousand – many of whom had simply stormed the gates without forking out the very affordable 4,05 East German Marks for a ticket! Opening with 'Nova Lepidoptera', the Barclays treated the crowd to a set of well over an hour and a half of material spanning most of their career. Bolstered by three guest musicians in the shape of Kevin McAlea, Bias Boshell and Colin Browne, the live sound was fuller than their most recent studio recordings. Songs including 'Medicine Man', 'African', 'Alone In The Night' and 'On The Wings Of Love' benefitted from a harder-edged delivery and powerful guitar solos from John, plus additional harmonies and keyboard arrangements. The volume was impressive, too, with two twenty-thousand Watt speaker stacks; for the second time in their history, the band's music crossed over the Berlin Wall – prompting complaints from the West about the noise from the East!

On the band's return to the UK, Ian Southerington and Gregg Jackman set to work at Advision Studios to mix the multi-tracks with input from the band (minus John, who was ill and unable to attend), and the entire concert was then delivered to Polydor for possible release as a live album. Unfortunately, double live albums were no longer in vogue, and it was decided to edit the material down to a single LP, cassette and CD's worth. To the annoyance of dedicated fans, though, the album's running order bore little relation to the actual sequence of songs at the concert, and for some bizarre reason, the CD and cassette even placed the bonus tracks after the real showstopping finale of 'Hymn', making for something of an anti-climax.

The working title for the album was *Back To The Wall*, which would have been entirely appropriate, but was eventually rejected in favour one of the Russian buzzwords then being bandied around by the media, *Glasnost*: the policy or practice of more open consultative government and wider dissemination of information. The album was released at the beginning of April, 1988, supported by a media campaign which included invaluable exposure on BBC 1, who showed forty minutes of highlights from the concert on Easter Sunday, and a video release on VHS and Betamax cassettes followed at the end of May. In spite of the marketing efforts, sales were disappointing, possibly because it was BJH's fourth live album in fourteen years, but in Germany, it just managed to crack the Top 50, and in the Swiss charts it made the Top 30. In 2013 the entire concert was rescued from the vaults and restored in its original running order on a remastered 2CD set by Esoteric Recordings, allowing fans to hear the gig as those East Berliners would have done, over twenty-five years ago, shortly before the Wall came down for good.

BBC In Concert 1972 (2002)

'Mocking Bird'; 'Medicine Man'; 'Galadriel'; 'Summer Soldier'; 'The Poet'; 'After The Day'; 'Moonwater'; 'Dark Now My Sky'.

Recorded at: The Paris Theatre, London, 16 November 1972
With the Barclay James Harvest Symphony Orchestra, leader Richard Studt, conductor Martyn Ford
Producer: Jeff Griffin
Sleeve Design: created by Philip Lloyd-Smee at Waldo's Design & Dream Emporium, and in keeping with EMI's 2002 remasters of the band's Harvest-era studio albums, the CD artwork shows an antique desk strewn with contemporary band memorabilia, including a concert programme from one of the band's 1970s orchestral tours.
Released: 27 May 2002, EMI

Somewhat surprisingly, no recordings of Barclay James Harvest playing live with the orchestra were released during their tenure with EMI, with the result that this BBC broadcast acquired legendary status amongst fans of the band. *In Concert* was a weekly programme highlighting contemporary artists performing live in the BBC's own Paris Theatre in London's Lower Regent Street. The theatre, formerly a small cinema, seated an invited audience of around three hundred, and the relatively small size of the stage limited the number of members of the orchestra on this occasion to between twenty and thirty. The concerts were not recorded onto multi-track tape (which would have enabled the sound engineers to mix the sound before broadcast), but were output directly to quarter-inch tape, with the balance done on the fly during the performance, quite a feat given the number of musicians on stage.

The Barclay James Harvest concert, introduced by Radio One DJ Alan Black, is a glorious performance, brilliantly capturing the exuberance and magic of orchestra and band in perfect fusion. It isn't always note-perfect, but this is real live music, with no retrospective overdubs and 'corrections'. Woolly later said that it was a case of, 'Forgive them, for they know not what they do!', but fondly described the end result as, 'Chaotic and tumultuous, but charming.' For domestic broadcast, the BBC's in-house engineers recorded in mono, but at the same time, their colleagues in the BBC Transcription Service took a separate line feed from the microphones and instruments and recorded in stereo, doing their own balance. The stereo recordings were then edited down to fit on a specially pressed LP record which was licensed for broadcast by radio stations around the world, in particular America. In the case of BJH, the introductions were omitted, the running order amended, and 'Mockingbird' and 'The Poet' shortened. Needless to say, these commercially unavailable 'transcription discs', which theoretically remained the property of the BBC, became much sought after on the collectors' market – until both the mono and stereo versions were finally released three decades later by EMI as a limited 2CD set. Once that edition had sold out, it was replaced by a single disc of the mono version only.

Other Official Live Recordings

A number of other live performances have seen the light of day down the years; not live albums *per se*, but nonetheless well worth seeking out. A couple of these made their first appearances as videos, in the now-defunct VHS or Betamax formats. The band's biggest indoor U.K. concert, which took place at London's Wembley Arena on 13 October 1984 in front of an audience of around 8,000, was filmed. Eleven tracks from the show were broadcast on TV, complete with dodgy conceptual footage filmed on Lindisfarne Island off the Northumbrian coast, and subsequently released as the *Victims Of Circumstance* video. The risible storyline rather detracts from the music, but fortunately, in 2012 the audio from the Wembley recordings was restored from the original multitracks and added as a bonus disc to the Esoteric label remastered CD of *Victims Of Circumstance*. Similarly, the Esoteric remasters of *Welcome To The Show* and *Caught In The Light* also come with bonus discs, in this case, the two halves of a complete concert recorded at The Town And Country Club in Kentish Town, London, on 16 February 1992 as part of the band's 25th Anniversary U.K. Tour. A ninety-minute edited version of the concert had already appeared on a VHS video entitled *The Best Of Barclay James Harvest Live*, and a fifty-minute broadcast version subsequently came out on DVD and a CD, without any input or approval from the band members, but the remastered CDs saw the entire concert released for the first time, and in remastered quality, to boot! Also worth seeking out is a DVD of the documentary film *Caught Live*, which captures the German leg of the band's 1977 tour in support of the *Gone To Earth* album. It must be said that the sound and picture quality of the DVD, which was mastered from an old cinema print, is less than top-notch, but it's still a great record of life on and off stage on tour, cut with wit and humour. Some of the recordings made on that tour were used as part of the *Live Tapes* album, and clearly, those are of much better sound quality.

Completists will also want to track down *After The Day: The Radio Broadcasts 1974-1976*, a 2CD set of all previously unreleased recordings from the BBC archives, released by Polydor/Universal in 2008. The first disc features an *In Concert* programme recorded at the Golders Green Hippodrome in London on 19 June 1974, including 'She Said', which was not broadcast at the time. The second CD comprises session recordings made for John Peel's and Bob Harris's Radio One programmes, two tracks recorded live for the *Old Grey Whistle Test* and four songs recorded in concert at the Liverpool Empire on 14 October 1976, originally released on a not-for-sale transcription disc LP in the BBC's series.

Finally, a mention for the band's first ever singles chart entry, the *Live EP* issued in March 1977 and including 'Rock 'N' Roll Star' and 'Medicine Man', the latter split across the two sides of the $33^{1/3}$ r.p.m. seven inch disc. Released in a picture sleeve limited to the first 10,000 copies, the EP is fondly remembered by many fans, but not many will know that in 1990 there were plans to reissue it as a CD single. The project got as far as artwork design and the printing of 'Cromalin' proofs, but sadly was then dropped. Fortunately, the recordings from the EP are available elsewhere, 'Rock 'N' Roll Star' on the *Live Tapes* album, and the full, unsundered version of 'Medicine Man' on the *Endless Dream* rarities compilation and the Polydor remastered CD of *Gone To Earth*.

Solo Work and Up To Date ...

Back in late 1972, with Barclay James Harvest undertaking an ever-increasing number of live engagements in an attempt to pay off some of their large debts to EMI, and their plans to record an ambitious double album stymied by the record company, morale within the band was at an all-time low. The *Four Winds* project would have comprised one side each of the band members' musical ideas, and, having been thwarted into rush-recording the single album *Baby James Harvest* instead, the musicians were even more determined to find an outlet for their individual talents. As Les Holroyd told the *New Musical Express:*

> If we hadn't come up with the idea of doing solo albums, I think we might have split. It's difficult when you've got three people writing and you come to do an album together. Often a song that a particular member of the band comes up with loses its original conception in being arranged to fit Barclay James Harvest. The solo album will clear up these separate ideas. John has recorded his, and I'm going into the studios soon.

As things turned out, John Lees' album, *A Major Fancy*, was the only one of the projected solo albums to come to fruition at the time, and even that wasn't released as planned. The album was recorded in December 1972 at Abbey Road, using not the other members of BJH, but other musicians he'd got to know along the way, including most of 10cc, Rod Argent (The Zombies and Argent) and members of The Pretty Things. Freed from the constraints of the band, John took the opportunity to experiment with different styles and textures, resulting in an album with a more relaxed, jazzy feel. It's a most enjoyable diversion, and notable for including the very first recording of 'Child Of The Universe', a song which had previously been rejected for inclusion on Barclay James Harvest albums. Elsewhere, songs like the 'Untitled' series, 'Witburg Night' and 'Long Ships' see John exploring new territory and stretching his creativity to intriguing effect. Unfortunately, events overtook the scheduled release of the album in June 1973, when the band parted ways with the Harvest label, and it would be more than four years before it finally saw the light of day on the Harvest Heritage mid-priced imprint in July 1977. Frustrated by this, John made another attempt at solo work in 1974, under the auspices of the band's new record label, Polydor, with his 'backing band' consisting of Les Holroyd on bass, legendary slide guitarist B. J. Cole, and Mike Moran (who later scored a UK Eurovision entry and Top 20 hit with Lynsey de Paul!) on piano. The recordings comprised two cover versions, of The Eagles' 'Best Of My Love' and the Charles Scott Boyer song 'Please Be With Me' (popularised by Eric Clapton), plus his own composition, 'You Can't Get It'. This time the record, a single of the first and last tracks did actually get released – only to be withdrawn days later on the orders of senior record company executives, nervous about their expensive and newly-signed band potentially splintering into solo acts. The only other John Lees solo recording to have been issued outwith the Barclay James Harvest umbrella was an untitled demo, recorded in around 1984, and issued on a fan club exclusive Christmas CD entitled *Strangely Mixed*. The song bears a slight resemblance to Bruce Springsteen's 'Hungry Heart', which may be why it didn't get used at the time, although John's explanation was much simpler: it hadn't come out 'because it's crap'! We prefer to say that it has a naïve charm ... All of John's solo output bar the latter demo were included on a double CD of *A Major Fancy* issued by Esoteric Recordings in 2010, which gathered up the remastered album, single cuts and unreleased material from John's personal tape collection.

Les Holroyd and Woolly Wolstenholme's projected solo projects never got beyond the writing stage, although one of Les's musical ideas for his own album ended up being developed into Barclay James Harvest's final single for the Harvest label, 'Rock And Roll Woman'. It was a source of immense frustration to Woolly that he was not only struggling to get his own compositions included on Barclay James Harvest albums (for example the unceremonious dumping of his 'Mæstoso' opus just before the release of *Everyone Is Everybody Else*), but he was also not permitted to take time out to make a solo record whilst remaining a member of the band. He was also increasingly unhappy about what he saw as band's abandonment of their English, classically-influenced roots in favour of a more American West Coast sound, and the pressures of large-scale tours were taking their toll, too. Matters came to a head in 1979 with Woolly's departure from Barclay James Harvest. At last he was free to make that long-planned solo album, working with two musicians he'd met while working, with the other members of Barclay James Harvest, on a multi-artist concept album and issued under the title *The Eye Of Wendor: Prophecies*, by Mandalaband. Guitarist Steve Broomhead and drummer Kim Turner were a perfect fit for Woolly's grand ideas, and the resulting *Mæstoso* album, released in October 1980 on the Polydor label, is a thing of beauty. The album incorporated both brand new compositions like 'Sail Away' (on his departure from BJH), the gorgeous 'A Prospect Of Whitby' and material, including the epic title track, 'Lives On The Line', 'Gates Of Heaven' and 'American Excess', which had been originally written for Barclay James Harvest. The band, augmented by bassist Terry Grady, undertook a UK tour supporting Judie Tzuke, and a German outing as guests of Canadian band Saga. A follow-up album with the title *Black Box* was planned and got as far as several songs being recorded, but Polydor, alas, more interested in propelling his erstwhile bandmates to ever-greater success in Germany, and unimpressed by the sales figures for *Mæstoso*, pulled the plug. It would be more than fifteen years before Woolly Wolstenholme recorded again.

The indifferent response to the release of *River Of Dreams* in 1997 and the subsequent announcement that the band would be taking a sabbatical seemed to many to be the end of Barclay James Harvest, and, indeed, John Lees, Les Holroyd and Mel Pritchard would never work together again. Few would have guessed, though, that, in different guises, Barclay James Harvest would still be a going concern more than twenty years later.

To the delight of older fans who pined for the days of the original quartet, and Woolly's input, in particular, it was announced in June 1998 that John and

Woolly had teamed up again to record a new studio album. With the addition of an old friend of John's, Craig Fletcher, on bass, and his pal Kev Whitehead on drums, the core of a new band was complete. A record deal was secured by David Walker in tandem with his co-manager, Lindsay Brown, who was now working at Eagle Records. The use of the Barclay James Harvest name was a potential minefield, since in legal terms the band was a partnership, with no single member having exclusive rights to the name. The compromise solution thrashed out with David Walker was that both John and Les would have the opportunity to record an album under the unwieldy moniker Barclay James Harvest Through The Eyes of John Lees or Barclay James Harvest Through The Eyes Of Les Holroyd respectively. Woolly, unwilling to commit to a contract, would appear on John's album as a featured artist, although in reality, his input was as great, if not greater, than John's, especially on the writing side. Recorded at John's Friarmere Studios between April and November 1998, *Nexus* was released by Eagle in February 1999 and reflected the fact that the record deal had come with strings attached: they had stipulated that the album should include re-recordings of some classic BJH songs alongside new material.

The result was something of a hybrid. Woolly did his best to rearrange the old songs into something quite different from the original recordings, with varying degrees of success. Some fans regarded it as sacrilege to tamper with the classics, whilst others enthused over new, improved versions of songs like 'The Iron Maiden' and 'Titles'. The 'new' songs weren't all new, either, including three songs which had been written between the sixties and the eighties for Barclay James Harvest but never taken up. Nevertheless, the album included a couple of fine new Woolly Wolstenholme songs, including the majestic 'Float', while 'Star Bright', written by John in Portugal at the same time as 'Paraiso Dos Cavalos', proved to be a great lost Barclay James Harvest classic. The album, so different in tenor from *River Of Dreams*, was received best by British aficionados who had mourned Woolly's departure back in 1979, whilst being greeted with a degree of bemusement by fans who were keener on the later BJH albums. There was no doubting the ecstatic reception that the band received when they hit the road in 1999, supplemented by 'the lovely Jeff Leach' on additional keyboards. Fans were amazed to hear songs like 'Brother Thrush' and 'She Said' which hadn't had a live airing in almost a quarter of a century, and with Woolly's glorious Mellotron-playing to the fore, the shows were a resounding success. The *Revival – Live 1999* album is an excellent record of that triumphant comeback tour, particularly in its limited expanded version with four extra songs. Another very successful German tour followed in late 2000 to promote the *Revival* live album, and when three U.K. concerts could be slotted into the schedule in March 2001, the response was equally rapturous.

Then it was Les Holroyd's turn, and after some delay, he set to work with Mel Pritchard on drums, plus former BJH guest musician Mike Byron-Hehir (lead guitar), his ex-bandmate in the Manchester band Sad Café, Ian Wilson, on backing vocals, former Monroe singer Steve Butler, also on backing vocals, and keyboard player Steve Pigott. Recorded at Revolution Studios, where BJH had recorded *Welcome To The Show* more than ten years earlier, the appropriately named *Revolution Days* was released on a small independent label, M Records in February 2002. For the band name, Les rejected the previously agreed form of Barclay James Harvest Through The Eyes Of Les Holroyd, opting instead for Barclay James Harvest Featuring Les Holroyd. It's clear that Les was keener to continue with the nineties Barclay James Harvest sound than John and Woolly's more retrospective return to the glory days, and in that he succeeded, with a well-crafted album showcasing his own talents and some biting lyrics. Many assumed that these were a comment on what was evidently now the demise of the original band and listening to songs like 'It's My Life', 'Quiero El Sol' and the title track, it's hard to disagree. Les wasn't immune from the pressure to include old Barclay James Harvest songs, too, and a new recording of his biggest hit, 'Life Is For Living', duly made the tracklisting. The album was well-received by diehard fans, especially in Germany, but its release was beset by distribution problems and financial issues, and it was rapidly deleted. A subsequent reissue with a different cover design added another remake, this time of 'Love On The Line'. Like John, Les now set out on tour in Germany, and the album *Live In Bonn* (actually recorded in Bad Godesberg, as the Bonn venue had burned down before the band got there!) is a record of that 2002 outing. BJHFLH, as we shall now call the band for the sake of brevity, continued to tour in Continental Europe, playing around fifty gigs in their first year, although none of those were on home territory.

Tragically, the U.K. fans would never see Mel Pritchard again: just a couple of days after his return from a four-day, five-concert series of BJHFLH guest slots at a big *Art On Ice* spectacular in Zürich, Mel was found dead at home on the morning of 28 January 2004. He'd suffered a heart attack, probably caused by an embolism. In truth, he hadn't been well for a while, with a second drummer being brought in for live concerts. There were even rumours that he hadn't actually played on *Revolution Days*, for which drummer Roy Martin, who later joined the touring band, is included in the 'special thanks' credits. In his heyday, Mel was one of the best drummers around, a perfect fit for Barclay James Harvest, and he is still much missed.

Les made the difficult decision to continue touring without Mel, using just the one drummer, and BJHFLH have performed many live shows since then, including two tours with twenty-five members of The Prague Philharmonic Orchestra under the banner Classic Meets Rock – Symphonic Barclay, the first of which was recorded for a 2CD set, *Classic Meets Rock – Live*. A third live album, another 2CD set entitled *Retrospective*, appeared in 2016, and is of interest for the inclusion of two otherwise unavailable songs which the band had been playing live since 2007, namely 'Fly Away' and 'Tonight's Gonna Be The Night'. BJHFLH continue to tour regularly in Europe but have not appeared in the U.K. since four dates supporting Asia in 2005 and a longer tour in 2007. A follow-up studio album to 2002's *Revolution Days* is long overdue, but the nearest that we've come to that at the time of writing is an unfinished demo of a song called '1989' which was posted on social media in November 2019.

Meanwhile, John's appetite for touring and recording reached a nadir after the 2001 shows, and he rejected an offer from Eagle Records for a second studio album, partly because he was convinced that in the download age there wasn't a market for it, and partly because he had been hard hit by the premature death of his friend and manager, David Walker. It may also have been a factor that whilst Woolly was going through a hyper-creative spell and pushing hard for a new album, John was at a low ebb creatively, and seriously thinking about retiring altogether. Woolly sank into a bad bout of the depression which had haunted him for much of his life and was hospitalised for a while. On his return, he needed another outlet for the musical ideas which were bursting out of him. He got involved with new CD issues of his old Mæstoso material, including the aborted *Black Box* project, now issued in its original unfinished form as *Songs From The Black Box*, then later with a slightly different tracklist, as *Black Box Recovered*. It was probably this, which, whilst not enough in itself, gave him the idea to reconvene his other former band, Mæstoso. With guitarist Steve Broomhead back in the fold, supplemented by Craig Fletcher and Kev Whitehead from John's band, Woolly sallied forth on what was to be one of the most creative and rewarding spells of his entire career. A brand new Mæstoso studio album, *One Drop In A Dry World*, released by Eclectic Discs in May 2004, showed his songwriting muse to be as strong as ever, with a slew of great songs, from the epic ('Blood And Bones') to the exotic ('Souk', co-written with Steve Broomhead) to the emotional ('2 a.m.'). Fired up with enthusiasm once more, Woolly put his heart and soul into the album and rehearsals for a planned short U.K. tour to promote it. Regrettably, after an absence of more than twenty years, the band's pulling power was severely limited, and in the end, only one concert went ahead, at London's Mean Fiddler. The emotive, celebratory atmosphere of that unforgettable night is captured on the warts and all live CD, *Fiddling Meanly*.

Undeterred, Woolly set out to make another studio album, *Grim*, which may well be the Mæstoso band's finest moment, although to be fair, all of their albums, including *Mæstoso* itself, are of an extremely high standard. *Grim*, released in October 2005, showed the band maturing into a real unit, with original *Mæstoso* musician Kim Turner now back in the drum seat, and creative input from all of the band members. The breadth of musical styles is huge, yet the album still hangs together as a coherent whole. Lilting ditties such as 'Hebden Bridge' and 'Birds' earn their place as much as the prog-rock tour de forces of 'Through A Storm' and 'Harp + Carp' ('the mediæval monstrosity', as Woolly described it!).

What was destined to be the final Mæstoso album came out in November 2007, under the title *Caterwauling* – according to Woolly's madcap and surreal online blog, this was because the original artwork and working title, *The Last Flight Of The Grafenberg*, had been scrapped on the advice of lawyers! It's a difficult album to listen to in hindsight, full of the emotional turmoil which Woolly was going through, and yet it still manages to encapsulate beauty, pathos, compassion and even dark humour. 'Soldier Of Fortune', 'The Road To Nowhere', Steve Broomhead's 'Matilda Yarrow' and Kim Turner's writing collaboration with Woolly on 'Always' are all high points, whilst the unbearably poignant 'Shoes' features a beautiful viola solo from Caravan's Geoffrey Richardson.

During the writing and recording of *Caterwauling*, Woolly and Craig were kept busy juggling their time between two bands, because John Lees was active again, relaunching his band under the new name John Lees' Barclay James Harvest. A longer U.K. tour in 2006, immortalised on the excellent live CD and DVD *Legacy – Live At The Shepherds Bush Empire*, was followed by dates in Greece and promotional appearances in Italy, with keyboardist Mike Bramwell substituting for Jeff Leach, who was fully occupied as a member of the house band in the West End musical, *We Will Rock You*.

Another live outing in 2009 saw John Lees' Barclay James Harvest, or JLBJH for short, treading the boards in the U.K., Germany, Holland, France and the U.S.A. (the latter a one-off appearance at RoSFest in Philadelphia), performing a much-changed set including more rarely-heard numbers from the extensive BJH catalogue, such as 'Early Morning', 'Summer Soldier' and 'In Search Of England'. These shows introduced a new, permanent second keyboard player, in the shape of the affable and very talented Jez Smith. The following summer they were the headliners at the Douro Rock and Blues Festival in Porto, Portugal – a perfect gig in a beautiful riverside setting. It was to be Woolly's last ever concert.

On his return from the Porto show, the depression which had laid him low and caused him to become suicidal on several previous occasions struck again with a vengeance. As the illness took hold, he made first one and then another unsuccessful attempt at ending it all, the latter of which resulted in him being sectioned and hospitalised in London. With several U.K. concerts, including a prestigious intimate event at London's Metropolis Studios for TV broadcast and later CD/DVD release, scheduled for just a few weeks away, the band had some difficult decisions to make. Woolly himself said that the gigs should go ahead without him, so, reluctantly, the show went on. Woolly's 'Poor Wages', 'The Poet' and 'Ursula (The Swansea Song)' were included in a hastily rearranged set, with 'Ursula' dedicated to him in his absence, and against all the odds the concerts were a great success. The euphoria was short-lived. On 13 December 2010, Woolly lost the final battle against his depression and took his own life, breaking the hearts of those who knew and loved him.

Another concert had been booked for 19 February 2011 at the Opera House in Buxton. After much heart-searching, John and the remaining musicians decided to continue with the band and go ahead with the gig as a tribute to Woolly. The 'BJH family' of fans who fought their way through the snow got the band through an incredibly difficult and emotionally-charged evening, turning the gig into both a wake and a celebration, a fitting farewell to a hugely talented and much-loved friend.

After Buxton, the band tentatively found their way into gigging without Woolly with a series of one-off festival appearances, including the High Voltage Festival in London's Victoria Park, where fans were able to pre-order a recording taken direct from the mixing desk on the day, picking it up very shortly after the end of the set. This raw and untouched live record was later issued commercially as *High Voltage, Recorded Live – July 23rd 2011*.

In a strange way, Woolly's tragic death gave John the impetus finally to get to work writing and recording again. The result was perhaps the finest of all the post-split projects, a collection of all-new songs entitled *North*. The closeness of the band members and their musical empathy shines through on an album which stands up there with anything recorded by the original Barclay James Harvest. Two songs, in particular, stand out, and have become live favourites: the title track is one, with its wonderful evocation of the band's home stamping grounds, charting the progress of one man from the cradle to the grave, its joyous chorus brilliantly capturing the splendour of the landscape when the sun (occasionally!) comes out. The other is a moving, heartfelt song summation of all of the band members' thoughts about Woolly, given the title 'On Leave' after John received a Christmas card from Woolly with that inscription, the day after he died. The album cover, a beautiful image of the sun setting over the Pots And Pans war memorial on Saddleworth Moor, matches the content within perfectly, and the album itself was rightly hailed as a magnificent latter-day addition to the BJH catalogue. As an added incentive, a limited deluxe edition of *North* came with a bonus disc of nine songs recorded live at the poignant Buxton concert which had marked fans' farewell to Woolly.

John Lees' Barclay James Harvest continued to play live and to explore new territory, playing not just in the U.K. and Germany, but travelling as far as Japan for the first concerts in that country by any version of Barclay James Harvest, and appearing with an orchestra in the stunningly dramatic setting of the Herodes Atticus Amphitheatre in the shadow of the Parthenon in Athens. At the time of writing, a brand new studio album is well underway. Sadly, the completion of that, and plans for more festivals and concerts, were put on hold, like everything else, by the 2020 COVID-19 virus outbreak. Not to be totally silenced, John uploaded a video of himself performing an updated, topical version of 'Hymn' on social media, which at the time of writing had reached more than sixty-eight thousand people!

Continued interest in the music of Barclay James Harvest in all its forms is amply demonstrated by the popularity of new, remastered editions of their considerable catalogue and that of Woolly Wolstenholme and Mæstoso. The latter's 2018 seven-disc box set, *Strange Worlds*, compiled by ourselves, included not only all of the original Mæstoso albums, but also a full album bonus disc with the unreleased recordings, demos and fragments which were Woolly's legacy to us.

The time seems right for a reappraisal of Barclay James Harvest's contribution to the world of rock music: intelligent, melodic and unique, their pastoral brand of progressive music has ploughed a singular furrow, and for that we will always treasure them.

Selected Solo and Post-1997 Album Discography

John Lees

A Major Fancy (Harvest SHSM 2018, July 1977, vinyl LP)
Untitled No.1 – Heritage; Child Of the Universe; Kes (A Major Fancy); Untitled No.2; Sweet Faced Jane; Witburg Night; Long Ships; Untitled No.3

A Major Fancy (Remastered 2CD, Esoteric ECLEC 22233, November 2010)
Untitled No.1 – Heritage; Child Of The Universe; Kes (A Major Fancy); Untitled No.2; Sweet Faced Jane; Witburg Night; Long Ships; Untitled No.3; Untitled No. 8 (previously unreleased song); Child Of The Universe (first version); Witburg Night (first mix); Untitled No. 2 (first version); Untitled No. 1 – Heritage (first version); Best Of My Love; You Can't Get It; Please Be With Me; Child Of The Universe (single edit)

Woolly Wolstenholme and Mæstoso

Woolly Wolstenholme – *Mæstoso* (Polydor 2374 165, October 1980)
Sail Away; Quiet Islands; A Prospect Of Whitby; Lives On The Line; Patriots; Gates Of Heaven (14/18); American Excess; Mæstoso – A Hymn In The Roof Of The World; Waveform (+ Even The Night – live in Vienna; Has To Be A Reason – live in Vienna on 2006 Eclectic Discs CD remaster)

Woolly Wolstenholme – *Songs From The Black Box* (Voiceprint VP174CD, June 1994)
Has To Be A Reason; Down The Line; All Get Burned; Too Much, Too Loud, Too Late; Even The Night; Deceivers All; The Will To Fly; Sunday Bells; Open; Sail Away; Quiet Islands; A Prospect Of Whitby; Lives On The Line; Patriots; Gates Of Heaven (14/18); American Excess; Mæstoso – A Hymn In The Roof Of The World; Waveform

Woolly Wolstenholme – *Black Box Recovered* (Eclectic ECLCD 1007, February 2004)
Deceivers All (different mix); Has To Be A Reason; Down The Line; All Get Burned; Too Much, Too Loud, Too Late; Even The Night; The Will To Fly; Sunday Bells; Open; Why Remain; Sail Away – Demo; A Prospect Of Whitby – Demo; Patriots – Demo; Quiet Islands – Demo; American Excess – Live; Lives On The Line – Live; Deceivers All – Live; Bootham Park Elegy

Mæstoso – *One Drop In A Dry World* (Eclectic ECLCD 1008, May 2004)
The Bells, THE BELLS!; Blood And Bones; A Waiting Game; It's You (Sixties Mix); Souk; One Drop In A Dry World; ANSS; The End Of The Road; Explorers; 2 a.m.; The Starving People Of The World All Thank You For Your Time; Carpet (+ It's You (the over-sixties mix); Flip; Music for The Wind In The Willows; The Starving People... – short version; Requiem from Blood And Bones; It's You – Eighties demo; A Waiting Game – different version with Craig Fletcher on vocals; The Angelus; Camelherd Hit By Falling Building on limited edition with bonus disc 'Second Splash')

Mæstoso – *Fiddling Meanly, live* (Eclectic ECLCD 1019, February 2005)
Abendrot; The Bells, TH BELLS!, Deceivers All; Has To Be A Reason; In Search Of England; The Iron Maiden; Sunday Bells; Poor Wages; The Poet/After The Day; The Will To Fly; A Prospect Of Whitby; Harbour; Early Morning; Big Organ End

Mæstoso – *Grim* (Eclectic ECLCD 1029, October 2005)
Coming Soon To A Cinema Near You; Through A Storm; Love Is ...; A Lark; That's The Price You Pay; The IceMan Cometh; Hebden Bridge; Loot; Harp And Carp; Birds; Location, Location, Location; Abendrot; Marsch Burleske; Pas de Deux; A Scene From A London Flat

Mæstoso – *Caterwauling* (Esoteric Recordings ECLEC 2017, November 2007)
Caterwauling; Soldier Of Fortune; The Road To Nowhere; Matilda Yarrow; The Collector; Closure; Always; I Don't Like You; Tonight Could Be The Night; Shoes; Strange Worlds; Quicksand; Blossom Hill; Pills

Woolly Wolstenholme (& Mæstoso) – *Strange Worlds* (Esoteric ECLEC 72636, July 2018, 7CD set)
Mæstoso (full album plus two live bonus tracks)
Black Box Recovered (full album)
One Drop In A Dry World (full album)
Fiddling Meanly – live at The Mean Fiddler (full album)
Grim (full album)
Caterwauling (full album)
The Unlost Works – demos and fragments: Your Starter For Ten; The Streets of This Town; Brian Maclean; The Angelus; Faith, Hope and Charity; Hiraeth; The Light at the End of the World; Wagon; Madrigal; A Stolen Life; Alone; Bill Song; A Funny Kind of Blue; Day Song; Sleeping; Romanze; It's a Dream (Robbie's Song); Winter World (for Chloe); Bethlehem; Death in Oldham

Barclay James Harvest Through The Eyes Of John Lees

Nexus (Eagle EAGCD052, February 1999)
Festival!; The Iron Maiden; Brave New World; Hors d'Oeuvre; Mocking Bird; Sitting Upon A Shelf; Hymn; The Devils That I Keep; Titles; Float; Loving Is Easy; Star Bright

Revival – Live 1999 (Eagle EAGCD120, March 2000)
A Devilish Intro; She Said; Festival!; For No One; The Iron Maiden; Hors d'Oeuvre; Mocking Bird; Harbour; River Of Dreams; Poor Man's Moody Blues; New Song (Old Story); Brave New World; Galadriel; Loving Is Easy; Star Bright (+ Suicide?; Brother Thrush; Mr. E; Hymn on limited tour edition)

John Lees' Barclay James Harvest

Legacy – Live at the Shepherds Bush Empire, London 2006 (Esoteric ECLEC2010, November 2007)
Valhalla; For No One; Child Of The Universe; The Iron Maiden; The Great 1974

Mining Disaster; Poor Man's Moody Blues; Suicide?; Medicine Man; In Search Of England; Poor Wages; Mocking Bird; The Poet/After The Day; Hymn

High Voltage, Recorded Live – July 23rd 2011 (Concert Live CLCD358, December 2011)
Nova Lepidoptera; Poor Wages; She Said; Galadriel; Ball and Chain; Mockingbird; Taking Some Time On; Medicine Man; Song for Dying; The Poet; After The Day; Hymn

Recorded Live In Concert At Metropolis Studios, London (Salvo SALVOSVX004, June 2012)
Nova Lepidoptera; Child Of The Universe; Poor Wages; Mockingbird; Summer Soldier; Poor Man's Moody Blues; Ursula (The Swansea Song); Ancient Waves; Medicine Man; The Poet; After The Day; Hymn

North (Esoteric Antenna EANTCD 21022, October 2013)
If You Were Here Now; Ancient Waves; In Wonderland; On Leave; The Real Deal; On Top Of The World; Unreservedly Yours; North; The End Of The Day (+ Ursula (The Swansea Song); Galadriel; Mockingbird; Ball And Chain; Summer Soldier; Medicine Man; Song For Dying; The Poet; After The Day on limited edition bonus disc, live at The Opera House, Buxton – 19th February 2011)

The Bloomsbury Theatre, London, 30th October 2009 (Lepidoptera LEPCD2001, May 2018)
Nova Lepidoptera; Child Of The Universe; Poor Wages; Mockingbird; The Iron Maiden; Cheap The Bullet; Poor Man's Moody Blues; Harbour; Galadriel; Summer Soldier; River Of Dreams; She Said; Suicide?; Hymn; The Poet; After The Day

The 50th Anniversary Concert (Lepidoptera 2CD/DVD, LEPCD3002, November 2018)
Mr. Sunshine; Child Of The Universe; She Said; Paraiso Do Cavalos / Sideshow; The Iron Maiden; In My Life; North; In Memory Of The Martyrs; The Acoustic Medley: Delph Town Morn/One Night/Mr.E/Guitar Blues/Just A Day Away/ Unreservedly Yours; River Of Dreams; On Leave; Taking Some Time On; Summer Soldier; Medicine Man; Mockingbird; Crazy City; The Poet / After The Day; Early Morning; Hymn
New studio album planned for release in 2021 ...

Barclay James Harvest Featuring Les Holroyd

Revolution Days (M MREC001, February 2002)
It's My Life; Missing You; That Was Then... This Is Now; Prelude; January Morning; Quiero El Sol; Totally Cool; Life Is For Living; Sleepy Sunday; Revolution Day; Marlene (from the Berlin Suite) [+ Love On The Line on 2003 Pure Music reissue]

Live in Bonn, 30th October 2002 (Pure Music 219-0102-0022, October 2003)
It's My Life; Revolution Day; Yesterday's Heroes; Prelude; January Morning; Rock 'N' Roll Star; The Song (They Love To Sing); Life Is For Living; Marlene

Classic Meets Rock Live (Kultopolis GmbH, 5051278/5051279, December 2006)
The Song (They Love To Song) – orchestra only; Crazy City – orchestra only; Prelude; January Morning; Back In The Game; Yesterday's Heroes; Rock 'N' Roll Star; Mockingbird; Hold On; Berlin; Ring Of Changes; Play To The World; That Was Then ... This Is Now; Life Is For Living; Hymn; Love On The Line; Shadows On The Sky

Retrospective (live) (Goldencore Records/Zyx GCR 20106-2, February 2016)
Intro; Who Do We Think We Are; The Time Of Our Lives; Victims Of Circumstance; Sip Of Wine; Ring Of Changes; Welcome To The Show; Crazy City; Poor Boy Blues; Friend Of Mine; Fly Away; Love On The Line; That Was Then ... This Is Now; Tonight's Gonna Be The Night; Hymn; Life Is For Living